The Essential Friends of Libraries

Fast Facts, Forms, and Tips

SANDY DOLNICK

AMERICAN LIBRARY ASSOCIATION
Chicago 2005

While extensive effort has gone into ensuring the reliability of information appearing in this book, the publisher makes no warranty, express or implied, on the accuracy or reliability of the information, and does not assume and hereby disclaims any liability to any person for any loss or damage caused by errors or omissions in this publication.

Composition by ALA Editions in Avenir and Galliard using Quark XPress 5.0 on a PC Platform

Printed on 50-pound white offset, a pH-neutral stock, and bound in 10-point coated cover stock by Victor Graphics

The paper used in this publication meets the minimum requirements of American National Standard for Information Sciences—Permanence of Paper for Printed Library Materials, ANSI Z39.48-1992. ∞

Library of Congress Cataloging-in-Publication Data

Dolnick, Sandy.
    The essential friends of libraries : fast facts, forms, and tips / Sandy Dolnick.
       p. cm.
    ISBN 0-8389-0856-X (alk. paper)
    1. Friends of the library—United States—Handbooks, manuals, etc. I. Title.
Z681.7.U5D65 2004
021.7—dc22   2004013275

Copyright © 2005 by the American Library Association. All rights reserved except those which may be granted by Sections 107 and 108 of the Copyright Revision Act of 1976.

Printed in the United States of America

09   08   07   06   05   5   4   3   2   1

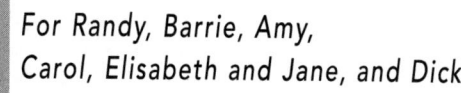
For Randy, Barrie, Amy,
Carol, Elisabeth and Jane, and Dick

Contents

Preface *xiii*
Acknowledgments *xv*

FAST FACTS FOR FRIENDS IN A HURRY 1

Academic Friends 1
Accounting 2
Advocacy 2
Affiliations 3
Agenda 3
American Library Association 4
Annual meeting 5
Appraisals 5
Audit 5
Authors 6
Awards 6
Bank accounts 7
Banner 7
Best practices 8
Board job descriptions 8
Board meeting 9
Board members, recruiting 9
Board of directors 10
Bonding of employees 11
Book clubs 11
Book sales 11

Book sales, customer retention   12
Book sales, dealers as volunteers   13
Book sales, dealers at   13
Book sales, donation of books for   14
Book sales, etiquette   14
Book sales, leftovers   14
Book sales, media attention   15
Book sales, merchandising   15
Book sales, online auction   16
Book sales, online fixed-price   17
Book sales, preparation for   18
Book sales, previews for Friends members   18
Book sales, pricing books   19
Book sales, pricing policy   20
Book sales, publicity for   20
Book sales, selling online   21
Book sales, smelly books   21
Book sales, sorting for   21
Book sales, volunteers   22
Bookmarks   23
Bookstores   23
Branch Friends   23
Brochures   24
Budgets   24
Bulk mail   26
Bylaws   26
Capital campaigns   27
Cause-related marketing   27
Center for the Book   28
Charter members   28
Citywide Friends   29
Codes of conduct   29
Coffee shops   30
Commitment   30

CONTENTS vii

Committees *31*
Community involvement *31*
Constitution *32*
Contracts *32*
Control *33*
Corporate support *33*
Correspondence *33*
Craft projects *34*
Demographics *34*
Development office *34*
Diversity *35*
Document storage *36*
Donations *37*
Due diligence *38*
Dues *38*
EIN number *39*
Elections *39*
Embezzling *39*
Endowments *40*
Evaluation of programs *40*
Executive committee *41*
Executive director *41*
Finances *41*
Financial disclosure *42*
Fiscal policy *42*
Fiscal year *43*
Flowchart *43*
Foundations *43*
Friends of Libraries U.S.A. (FOLUSA) *44*
Fund-raising *45*
Fund-raising, prospect list for *45*
Genealogy *46*
Gift baskets *46*
Gift policy *47*

Gift shops   47
Goals   48
Grants   48
Grievances   49
Historian   49
Honorary members   49
Hospitality   50
Incorporation   50
Insurance policies   51
Internet   51
Issue statement   52
Junior Friends   52
Letter writing   52
Library director   53
Library Legislative Day   53
Literacy   54
Literary Landmarks   54
Lobbying   54
Logo   55
Maintenance   56
Marketing   56
Media   57
Meeting costs   57
Meetings   58
Membership   58
Membership, lapsed   59
Membership renewal form   60
Memorial   60
Minutes   60
Mission statement   61
Murder in the Library   62
National promotions   62
Newsletter   62
Nominating committee   63

Nonprofit status   64
Office support   66
Parades   67
Partners, business   67
PayPal   68
Perks   68
Planning   68
Positioning   68
President   69
Programs   70
Programs, book-related   70
Public service announcements   71
Publications   72
Publishers' websites   73
Quorum   74
Raffles   74
Recognition   75
Record keeping   75
Resources   76
Resumes   77
Rewards   77
Scholarships   78
Secretary   78
Software   78
Speakers, fees for   79
State and local requirements   79
State Friends of Libraries   80
State libraries   80
Steering committee   81
Strategic planning   81
Successful Friends Policy   81
Sunshine laws   82
Talent show   83
Tax exemption   83

Technology   *83*
Teen Friends   *84*
Term of office   *84*
Treasurer   *85*
Tributes   *86*
Trustees   *86*
Vice president   *87*
Volunteers   *87*

Appendix A: Resource Websites for Friends   *89*
Appendix B: State Friends of Libraries Organizations   *92*
Bibliography   *99*

CD CONTENTS

Folder 1: Running a Board
1-1 Sample agenda—annual meeting and regular meeting
1-2 Sample agenda—board of directors meeting
1-3 FOL proposed budget
1-4 Job description for bookstore manager
1-5 Sample job description for executive director
1-6 Letter of agreement for executive director
1-7 Sample list of purchases for the fiscal year
1-8 Board of directors positions
1-9 Proposed guidelines for branch Friends
1-10 Proposal for relationship guidelines
1-11 Sample minutes, board meeting
1-12 Checklist for strategic planning
1-13 Checklist for advocacy
1-14 How to organize a media center/school library FOL

Folder 2: Nomination Process
2-1 About the Friends
2-2 Board criteria grid
2-3 Prospective board member information form
2-4 Nominating committee schedules and form letters
2-5 Application for student board member
2-6 How to organize a teen FOL

Folder 3: Publications

3-1 Friends of Pikes Peak Library District newsletter
3-2 Friends of Tippecanoe County Library newsletter
3-3 FOLUSA sponsors
3-4 Friends of Washoe County Library brochure
3-5 Appraisal day

Folder 4: Donations and Membership

4-1 Letter to recipient describing donations in honor
4-2 Thank-you letter for business membership
4-3 Thank-you letter to donor
4-4 How to organize a Friends foundation

Folder 5: Book Sales

5-1 Sixteen ways to make more money at your book sale
5-2 Book sale floor plan
5-3 Guide to location of books
5-4 Thank-you letter for book donation
5-5 "This is a friendly book sale" rules

Folder 6: Volunteer Management

6-1 Thank-you letter to volunteer
6-2 Volunteer program and procedures handbook
6-3 Volunteer's receipt of handbook
6-4 Volunteer application
6-5 Student volunteer application
6-6 Employee and volunteer emergency information

Folder 7: Programs

7-1 A tisket, a tasket
7-2 Murder mystery
7-3 The drill team experience
7-4 Drill team information
7-5 Making money and making Friends
7-6 Flowchart for planning an author lecture event
7-7 How to book an author
7-8 Event checklist
7-9 Sample report sheet for event evaluation
7-10 Register of Literary Landmarks

7-11 Designating a Literary Landmark
7-12 Getting involved with literacy programs
7-13 Holding a read-a-thon

Folder 8: Legal Necessities

8-1 Sunshine law top 10
8-2 Sunshine laws
8-3 Articles of incorporation
8-4 Mission statement
8-5 Bylaws
8-6 Raffle—Colorado
8-7 Raffle—North Carolina
8-8 IRS Form SS-4—application for Employer Identification Number

Folder 9: Policy Manuals

9-1 Code of ethics
9-2 Development and fund management policy of the gift and endowment program
9-3 Code of regulations
9-4 Policies and procedures

Preface

During the last twenty-five years I've answered many questions about Friends of the Library. Often I've heard the same questions over and over again. I helped answer them as best I could in the three editions of that durable seller, the *Friends of Libraries Sourcebook*.

The *Sourcebook* was originally written prior to many of the changes that have occurred in this electronic age, and while it certainly filled the demand and met a very real need, it could not make accessible all of the information and help that I am now able to offer with this combination of reference book and CD.

The questions have kept coming, but in the last five years before my retirement, I began to notice something different about them. People would call in a hurry, anxious to have a specific question answered quickly before a meeting. They often said they loved the *Sourcebook* but didn't have time to look up the information they needed. I used to keep a list of frequently asked questions and answers at the front desk of the Friends of Libraries U.S.A. (FOLUSA) office so they could be easily answered by others.

These wonderful people who were calling were very harried volunteers, who out of the goodness of their hearts had taken on a position with the Friends. Sometimes they were librarians who had to cope with Friends in a situation not taught in library school. Trustees would call, unsure of their position in relation to the Friends. Once in a while, a question represented a problem that had just pushed someone to the brink. My favorite was a call from someone who had been elected president, was unfamiliar with running a board meeting, and wanted to know how to conduct one and what should be discussed. This book is for all of these callers and their successors.

This book consists of ready-reference articles that cover all aspects of Friends of the Library groups: organization, finances, personnel, fund-raising, programs, legalities, and so on. Cross-references to other relevant articles within the book are in boldface type. Certain articles in the book also cross-refer to relevant materials on the CD. The CD itself is arranged topically into nine folders, each of which contains various sample documents that will help a Friends group conduct the activities of their organization.

This book is more than just a ready-reference guide. It is personal in that I have not hesitated to voice my opinions, of which I have collected many in my time as a library Friend. These thoughts were honed by hearing the viewpoints of the different sides of each issue. I have learned a great deal from all of the Friends and librarians it was my pleasure to work with for almost thirty years, and I thank them for being so frank and open in their discussions. I was privileged to serve an ever-changing board of directors as executive director of FOLUSA, and my long tenure in this post was rich in experiences that showed the various demands made on Friends groups, libraries, suppliers, publishers, and trustees, and which illuminated the various problems our members face.

I don't want to make it seem as if I wrote this book all by myself. The opinions are mine, but I've called on many fine people and groups to amplify them, as is evident in the acknowledgments. I also want to thank Jane Rutledge for her support during my tenure, and for her generosity in supplying this book with her knowledgeable entries on book sales. ALA Editions has been hugely supportive of the Friends by publishing the series of *Sourcebooks* I've worked on, and in doing so has helped the cause of libraries.

I only hope that in this busy world of volunteers juggling family, work, and other demands on their time, opening this book will mean they'll find the support they need and deserve, even at the last minute.

SANDY DOLNICK

Acknowledgments

Jane Rutledge, author of the "Book sale" entries, "Sixteen Ways to Make More Money," and much, much more. West Lafayette, Indiana

Friends of Connecticut Libraries

Marcia Barker, program coordinator, Friends of the Canton Public Library, Michigan

Carleen Sharpenberg, Friends of the Columbus Metropolitan Library, Ohio

Susan Schmidt, Friends of the Library, Montgomery County, Maryland

Annette Stith, executive director, Friends of the Pikes Peak Library District, Colorado

Louise Pinckney Courts, Friends of the Richland County Public Library, South Carolina

Sharon Honig-Bear, Friends of the Washoe County Library, Reno, Nevada

Lillian Levin, Friends of the Welles-Turner Memorial Library, Glastonbury, Connecticut. Materials from *Planning Library Friends' Book Sales,* second edition, © copyright 2000 by Lillian Levin, by permission of the author.

Sara C. Oates, Pennsylvania Citizens for Better Libraries

Sally Gardner Reed, executive director, Friends of Libraries U.S.A.

Beth Nawalinski, editor, FOLUSA's *News Update*

Library Book Cart Precision Drill Team Manual, © 2002 by Linda D. McCracken and Lynne Zeiher, by permission of McFarland and Company, Inc., Box 111, Jefferson, NC 28640, www.mcfarlandpub.com

Patrick Hogan, ALA Editions

And for the many Friends not individually listed from whom I've learned

FAST FACTS FOR FRIENDS IN A HURRY

ACADEMIC FRIENDS CD Reference: Running a Board

From the smallest college to the largest university, whether rich in endowments or poorly funded, Friends groups have formed to support the libraries of universities and colleges. The increased costs of keeping information current are especially difficult to meet in these institutions, and keeping the library visible to the campus community is also vital. Friends groups help to accomplish this. They may be composed of faculty, students, members of the surrounding community, and alumni. They may help build special collections, include private collectors whose collection would make a wonderful enhancement to the library, or have contacts within the community or faculty that will lead to donations. Unlike public library Friends, the library staff is often deeply involved in planning the Friends' program events. Officers may be elected in the Friends group, but they may play a more cursory role. The **development office** of the institution should work with the group to do mailings to alumni; it has been learned that many graduates or even those attendees who did not graduate will donate to the library rather than to a particular school. Academic Friends' programs may include simple discussions with faculty members, author programs, programs on book collecting, special publications from the library's collection with attendant fanfare, trips to local or foreign sites of interest, and awards to students and alumni. Development officers learn from each other at meetings of FOLUSA (Friends of Libraries U.S.A.), ALADN (Academic

Library Advancement and Development Network), and DORAL (Development Officers of Research Academic Libraries), among other groups.

ACCOUNTING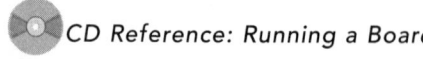
CD Reference: Running a Board

Accounting, or keeping track of your income and expenses, is one of the most important disciplines of a successful Friends group. With accounting and a **budget** it's easy to see how you are spending your money, and much of it is done in the expectation of membership money setting off the expenses. A **treasurer** is one of the first appointments a Friends group makes because of the need to keep track of where money is coming from and where it is spent. The treasurer may be a person with financial experience, an accountant, or a bookkeeper. The services of a certified public accountant will be necessary during the development and life of a group. Accounting applies not only to money but to goods and services which have monetary value. (See **Audit; Document storage; Finances**)

ADVOCACY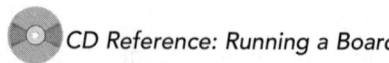
CD Reference: Running a Board

Advocacy is actually just being a Friend of the Library. By choosing that designation you are proclaiming your affinity with the library. By wearing a library T-shirt or carrying a library book bag you are sharing your views with the public. By sharing your enthusiasm for the library or the activities of the Friends with others you are being an advocate. As a citizen you are able to express your point of view in public, with state legislators and in public forums in your community. When you speak on behalf of the Friends you are prohibited from saying certain things you could say as an individual, and this is where Friends have to be careful because of the tax laws. One must separate one's own opinion, however correct, from the voice of a Friend of the Library when speaking as a Friend. As a citizen you can urge other people to vote a certain way or for a specific political candidate. As a Friend of the Library, however, you are not allowed to do this; you can explain which approach is most beneficial to the library, and what the effect of various options would be. When like-minded citizens get together, they can decide on a course of action. However, things have changed since de Tocqueville's famous quote:

> These Americans are the most peculiar people in the world. You'll not believe it when I tell you how they behave. In a local community in their country, a citizen may conceive of some need which is not being met.

What does he do? He goes across the street and discusses it with his neighbor. Then what happens? A committee begins to function on behalf of the need. You won't believe this, but it's true: all of this is done without reference to any bureaucrat. All of this is done by private citizens on their own initiative. (Alexis de Tocqueville, *Democracy in America*, 1835)

Nowadays you have to involve the bureaucrats. One has to keep in mind the strictures of the IRS regarding a Friends group's tax-exempt status as a 501(c)(3) organization. It's also useful to divide a special copy of your mailing list by voting districts. You will save time and effort by this type of arrangement. You'll be prepared in case of a special election, or in case of a get-out-the-vote effort that may affect the library, to ask specific districts to make their local representatives aware of the library's needs. (See **Letter writing; Lobbying; Nonprofit status**)

AFFILIATIONS

A Friends of the Library group can feel very isolated if it is not aware of its connections, or affiliations, with other organizations that exist in the local, regional, and national community. New Friends groups, or those that have started to get a little stale, should look for ways to refresh themselves by affiliating with other groups. Finances should not stand in the way of doing this; you may be able to attend meetings of other groups as a liaison, or a board member may wish to underwrite a membership if needed. The possibilities include countywide and statewide Friends of Libraries groups, Friends of Libraries U.S.A., Rotary clubs, Women's Clubs, chambers of commerce, PTAs, other local nonprofit groups, the local PBS station, and other groups that are important in your community. Your Friends group will profit from new ideas and opportunities to cooperate, but so will the other group(s) when they realize the potential the Friends represent. (See **Appendix B; State Friends of Libraries**)

AGENDA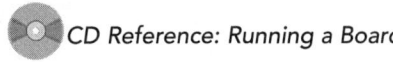

Agendas, the list of business that needs to be covered at a meeting, differ depending on the type of meeting they are meant to guide. All agendas must be flexible, since sometimes people who were supposed to make reports are not present, or have to leave or be late, so that their item on the agenda is moved to a more convenient time. An agenda for a typical monthly board of directors meeting can be fairly brief if there is no unusual business to discuss. This can be helpful, since it allows some open time that can accommodate creative discussions. Sometimes just hearing about a project someone is involved with at another organization can trigger ideas for your Friends group. A long agenda, which will take a long time to get through, can be helped along by having the number of minutes needed to present and discuss each item placed after its listing (i.e., 10 min.). A typical agenda usually includes the following items, with the name of the person giving the report following the item:

Call to order

Reading of the minutes followed by corrections, approval; or there may be a motion to dispense with the reading of the minutes if they were sent out by mail or e-mail ahead of time

Reports of officers, usually the president and treasurer

Committee reports

Old business, left over from a previous meeting

New business

Calendar or announcements if not given previously

Adjournment

An agenda for an **annual meeting** is an entirely different agenda than that for a monthly **board meeting.**

AMERICAN LIBRARY ASSOCIATION

The American Library Association, or ALA, is the largest national association for librarians in the United States. It has sections for librarians of all types: public, academic, special, school, and many other subgroups, including trustees. The ALA publishes many materials useful for public relations, including its famous posters, as well as bookmarks and incentive items. The Friends of Libraries U.S.A. (FOLUSA) is an affiliate of the ALA. FOLUSA has a kindred purpose with the ALA and regularly meets in conjunction with it to take advantage of the educational meetings and exhibits at the ALA's annual and midwinter conferences. These are held in major cities in various parts of the United States, to give opportunities to meet with different mixes of the American population. The Friends meetings at ALA conferences have grown extensively and have become a major morale booster and educational tool as they have broadened their fields of interest. (See **Appendix A; Friends of Libraries U.S.A.**)

ANNUAL MEETING

 CD Reference: Legal Necessities

The annual meeting is legally mandated in a Friends organization's constitution and bylaws and is held yearly to consider issues which affect the group, especially electing officers and board members, considering changes to bylaws, and anything else that might affect the organization's well-being. The minutes read are from the last annual meeting, one year previously. (There is usually a motion to dispense with the reading of these minutes.) The agenda is a brief summary of the financial year, income minus expenses, and current funds; a president's report of highlights; and a report from the nominating committee on new officers and board members that were nominated. Nominations from the floor can be accepted if they are allowed in the bylaws and there is a quorum present to vote. Old and new business and a call for a move to adjourn can bring an annual meeting to a close in less than fifteen minutes, if run with a strong hand. A special program that attracts a large audience generally follows an annual meeting. (See **Elections**)

APPRAISALS

An appraisal is an expert evaluation of the value of something. The popularity of some television shows has alerted audiences to unknown treasures in their attics. Friends groups have long invited book appraisers to visit at special times during an annual book sale, where they would appraise books for free, asking instead for a donation to the library from each customer. This appraisal process can be expanded to include antiques and specialists in silver, china, art, photographs, furniture, and collectibles. The dealers are able to meet potential clients, and the Friends and the library benefit from the increased attendance. An appraisal becomes a membership event if it's held for members only. (See **Book sales, dealers at**)

AUDIT

An audit is an in-depth look at an organization's financial records from the past year. It is a necessary exercise, especially as a Friends group grows in size. If your group is a recognized nonprofit organization (i.e., it has a federal EIN number), its audit records must be available to the public upon request. These records demonstrate that the group was fiscally responsible, that it has followed the mission statement, and that the funds spent were used to benefit the library. Even if an organization does not show a profit, it is important to keep records of the way money was spent. Many donors want to see an audit before giving money to an institution in order to be sure that those funds will be used wisely. An accountant (usually a certified public accountant) must perform the audit and sign it, stipulating its correctness. For a large Friends group, an outside firm must conduct the audit. To cut costs, a board member might know someone who can do it, or a large firm in the community might do it pro bono. Keeping meticulous records during the year (see **Accounting**) makes the audit process relatively painless. The information in the audit will be required for tax forms for that year, as well as for any applications for donations and grants.

AUTHORS

Authors can be the frosting on the cake for programs given at the library. They bring in a diverse, ready-made audience if their work has been published, as well as people just interested in the creative process. They come with built-in publicity. If they have reached celebrity status, even more people respond. It is a time-consuming task to plan author events; it is most helpful to begin the process by contacting publishers. Authors are aware of the huge debt they owe to libraries that buy their books and keep them available on the shelves long after the bookstores have forgotten them. Almost all have a favorite story to tell about the importance of libraries in their lives. They will usually respond to requests for autographs if you send them a book and return envelope, if it's to be used for an event on behalf of the library. It is also useful to keep in mind that authors do not have to still be living to contribute to the programming. A retrospective of a special author's work, either in an evening, over a weekend, or in study groups over a period of time can concentrate on newly appreciated works, hometown writers, or those celebrating milestones since their first work was published. There are many writers who were underappreciated in their time but who are found to be relevant by later audiences, or who have been forgotten but whose messages are once again important. (See **Programs, book-related; Publishers' websites**)

AWARDS

There are few easier ways for a local Friends group to increase its visibility and to thank people who have done good things for their library than to give awards. An award is a meaningful **recognition** of effort on behalf of a vital community resource, the library. It should be given in an appropriate ceremony and publicized to local and state media. An award can be given to recognize a generous donor or business, volunteers, library staff, etc. Specific awards can be given at certain times of the year, e.g., an award can be given to a local or state elected official (who has made a contribution to the library) during National Library Week; or to volunteers at a recognition event at the end of the program year. A thank-you can be said anytime, but an award is a lasting manifestation of gratitude. Some awards are named after special donors and can carry a cash gift. Some are plaques or certificates. A plaque can be hung in the library with a name added to it each year the award is presented. Some may expect a speech on a special topic to be part of the acceptance ceremony for an award. The Friends' president usually presents the award. Media coverage of the award ceremony is always useful. Popular annual award events held by Friends groups are dedicated to an author for a specific contribution; to a native son who has made good; or to a writer who has contributed to local or regional history, or to public affairs or historical research. The award given to the author, and the expenses for travel to the ceremony, are often covered by a special endowment. (See **Donations; Endowments; Rewards; Tributes**)

BANK ACCOUNTS

Your group's bank accounts should be established under the Friends of the Library name. The treasurer, the president, and as a safeguard, the accountant, should be registered as signers. Depending on the amount of money that is usually in the account, the board should decide if a savings or money market account is advisable. Factors to consider are money flow, interest rate, accessibility of funds, and safety. Book sales need money from the account for the expenses incurred by setting up the sale and for having change on hand. They also provide large amounts of cash that have to be promptly deposited, often in a night depository. (See **Fiscal policy**)

BANNER

A banner is one of the simplest ways to proclaim that the Friends exist and that it's time to join them. It should hang outside the library during fund-raising drives and National Library Week and can also be used in local parades and fairs. Banners are not expensive, considering how much use can be gotten from them. They make a nice potential donation from a business that either makes them or buys many of them for its own use. Banners are usually made of heavy-duty nylon, with grommets around them to make display easier. They may be purchased from flag and banner makers and sign makers.

BEST PRACTICES

"Best practices" is a business term that refers to developing a coherent plan for accomplishing the goals you set. To avoid misplacing energies in ways that are not productive, it is useful to practice **due diligence** and find out what has worked for other groups—what are the "best practices." This can pertain to fund-raising for both small and large amounts, publications, membership retention, involvement of the community, financial record keeping, finding board members, and other activities that are fundamental to the health and welfare of the organization. The network that you build to answer your questions will change depending on your needs, but the ability to find the answers to your questions is of inestimable value. Start a Rolodex or database and keep it up; don't hesitate to ask questions. Keep in mind that not everything that works in one environment or community translates well in another. Contacts in organizations often change, but the answers are still there. Surveys of your members may help you decide where to expend your energies. Don't forget that FOLUSA's newsletter, *News Update,* often includes examples of best practices.

BOARD JOB DESCRIPTIONS 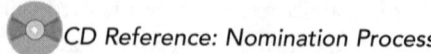 *CD Reference: Nomination Process*

Each member of the board of directors may be a chair or a member of a committee. The board president is considered an ex officio member of each committee. All prospective members of the Friends board of directors should know what is expected of them. They should be familiar with the mission of the group, the dates of board meetings, what their function will be on the board, and board member duties. They should also attend program meetings or other events besides the scheduled board events when possible. Their financial obligations should be made clear to them. If they are executives, it is helpful for them to know if they will be expected to use their staff or other company resources on the Friends' behalf. There may be directors who are not available during certain times of the year but are willing to help at other times. Be sure their availability will work with the board job descriptions assigned to them. The information they need should be kept in a notebook, or computer files pertaining to each special event should be copied for them. Passing on each year's accumulated wisdom, trials, and triumphs will make it easier for each new board chair to function. This makes it easier to find reputable suppliers and people who are willing to help with projects. It is also a nice board ceremony to have a chair pass on the notebook to the next chair of the committee.

BOARD MEETING

 CD Reference: Running a Board

Meetings of the **board of directors** are held on a regular basis, usually monthly except over the summer. It is important to identify those attending the meeting and have a large name card in front of each place, so everyone learns the others' names. The **agenda** should be sent out ahead of time to members of the Friends board and to the library director, so that those involved can be properly prepared. If handouts are required, be sure the **secretary** is informed and given the materials to collate properly for each member. The agenda can also be posted in the library. While businesslike, the Friends board often has a social aspect if the people in attendance have the time before or after it to share coffee and a treat, or meet somewhere for lunch or dinner for a special meeting. People may join these boards to meet those of similar interests, so they should have the opportunity to do so.

BOARD MEMBERS, RECRUITING

 CD Reference: Nomination Process

Recruiting members for the board of directors is an ongoing process. No matter how great you think your board is, someone will be leaving soon and there will be a vacancy. There should be a pool of names to consider of those who meet the general requirements for being a good board member: this list has been accumulated by other board members and librarians who have contact with the public. Sometimes a person has moved into the community and is interested in getting involved; these people can be a great resource because their new contacts and new interest in the group can help bring in fresh ideas. Setting up a position on the board that is filled by a high school student who is chosen by the high school principal or the student council is a good plan as well. It will look good on students' college applications and will make important connections for the group. A liaison from the local PTA/PTO and the Women's Club will also have a positive effect as a board member. The board must decide if a liaison position has voting rights if it is not covered in the bylaws. It usually does not. In an academic Friends group, there should be room for a student and a member of the faculty on the board. In these groups alumni usually make up the body of the board, but depending on the site of the campus, a "town" member may also be welcome. (See **Diversity; Nominating committee**)

BOARD OF DIRECTORS

 CD Reference: Running a Board

The board of directors of a Friends group is responsible for the guidance of the organization. The Friends group may be run by volunteers or by staff, and there may be an executive director who handles the day-to-day affairs, but the board of directors decides on the goals and objectives, both short- and long-term, that are a manifestation of the mission statement. Deciding on holding a book sale once a year to raise money for the library may be the sole activity of the group, or there could be many functions. These are decided upon by the Friends board working with the library director. The board meets at regular preannounced intervals to conduct business. These meetings are run by the board **president** within the format of parliamentary procedure, using *Robert's Rules of Order*, or the *Standard Code of Parliamentary Procedure* by Alice Sturgis. The meeting is open to the public because of the **sunshine laws,** except when discussing personnel issues or other issues of that type. There is usually little likelihood of anyone wanting to attend a board meeting except when invited. A member of the library staff should be invited, and there is usually someone designated for that purpose, either the director, the librarian in charge of public affairs, or another delegate. It is less typical to have a trustee attend regularly, since the library director can report back to the **trustees.** The size of the board is determined in the **bylaws** and is best done in a general way—"no less than fifteen members" or "no more than fifteen members"—so as not to make it difficult to fulfill. This number does not include ex officio positions. There should also be a statement of agreement by each Friends board member that they promise to follow the mission statement and will attend the meetings of the board, not missing more than two consecutive meetings unless excused for unusual circumstances. (See **Codes of conduct; Elections; President; Secretary; Treasurer; Vice president**)

BONDING OF EMPLOYEES

Bonding is insurance that protects an organization from illegal acts committed by its employees, such as embezzling. It can be a small rider added to existing insurance. Small Friends groups can be especially hard hit by theft and embezzlement because they can't afford extensive safeguards and aren't large enough to absorb the losses. If your group pays the wages of an employee who handles money and has checkbook and credit card access, it would be wise to have that person covered, no matter how well-known or likable they are. If your group is small, or your funds are handled by the library, you shouldn't have to worry about embezzling, though it's always important to have safeguards in place.

BOOK CLUBS

A book club is a regularly scheduled meeting of people who gather to discuss books that they have read. They may pursue an agenda of serious books or may be more informal in their reading program. The group can be as small as four or as large as thirty-five members. The traditional book club consisted of like-minded women; book clubs have been revived in recent years, and they may now include men or be made up of mothers and daughters. A wonderful boon for Friends, book clubs have brought a new audience to libraries and reading, and many potential members to Friends groups. The library is a natural focal point for these clubs, and the Friends can help sponsor various book clubs and set up meetings for other groups to swap multiple used books. Occasional programs aimed at these clubs or their leaders, discussions of various reading choices available, and making an author available to a club's members (via telephone hookup, Internet chat room, correspondence, videoconference, or lecture) are all ways to facilitate book clubs. The clubs could also view occasional movies related to books on their reading lists. The library should be able to order books for clubs at a discount, or partner with a local bookstore to provide a discount. (See **Programs, book-related**)

BOOK SALES
 *CD Reference: Book Sales*

A book sale raises funds for the library by selling used books culled from the library collection as well as book donations from the public. Book sales have a literature of their own, with websites and electronic discussion lists devoted to them (the FOLUSA-L list is a prime example). This topic deserves major attention, and can only be covered in a book like this by touching the high points and by the document samples you will find on the CD. The entries in this area were written by Jane Rutledge of Lafayette, Indiana, calling on her long experience not only as a book sale chair but as former editor of the FOLUSA newsletter, *News Update*.

It is important to note that book sales can be many different events in various locales. They can be a book cart set out on the floor with a cardboard sign, selling by the honor system, or a small cubicle with books on shelves selling for one dollar each, also on the honor system. Larger and more systematic sales may be held once a month or several times a year. There can be a large room dedicated to sales, where Friends have a regular schedule of staffing it for limited hours, and spend time sorting large numbers of books. There can be mammoth book sales held once a year, sometimes off-site in a special large setting, where thousands of books are sold and a good portion of the group's budget is made for the year. The public has come to expect to buy used books this way, and many make a habit of coming year after year, sometimes recycling the books previously purchased. It is hard work to produce a successful sale, and a wonderful community event. It is a good place to meet people, and should not be the preserve of a few regulars who like to do things their way. A book sale is a great place for new Friends members to feel needed, and to contribute time. Children can be put to work, Boy Scouts, Girl Scouts, and high school teens who can use some community involvement. Local politicians and celebrities can be involved, and an auction of more expensive items can be a part of the sale. Don't underestimate the amount of time a book sale can take, or the many benefits that can accrue from one.

BOOK SALES, CUSTOMER RETENTION

Some Friends groups ask customers at each book sale to sign up if they'd like to be on a mailing list for future sales. This is especially helpful if many customers come from outside the community where they may not routinely see the sale publicity. A postcard with the sale's dates, hours, and location is a quick and inexpensive way to reach interested people. If the next sale is already scheduled, it's easy to hand out bookmarks at the sale with the information about the next one. If possible, find a way to keep track of the number of sales made, to try and quantify the number of people in attendance.

BOOK SALES, DEALERS AS VOLUNTEERS

Asking book dealers to sort and price books or to help set up the book sale sets up a conflict-of-interest situation that most Friends groups prefer to avoid. Dealers will often offer their services, either as a community service or with the request that they receive the first chance to buy items of interest. While many book dealers are good Friends members and public-spirited citizens, it is best to avoid even the appearance of favoritism. Having a policy in place before the question arises is best.

BOOK SALES, DEALERS AT

Dealers can assist at book sales and help identify books that should receive special treatment, those rare finds that collectors want. Dealers can also suggest ways to divide the books at a sale into categories, and they can help you get rid of the leftovers when the sale is finished. If there is the chance that you have found a rare or unique volume, you can have your book appraised by an antiquarian book dealer, who would be listed on the Antiquarian Booksellers of America website at http://www.abaa.org/find-bookseller/booksellersearch.cgi. (See **Appraisals**)

Dealers who sell used books use Friends book sales as a way of finding stock at reasonable prices, and often book dealers will be your best customers. However, dealers and book scouts have developed a bad reputation at book sales, often indulging in competitive and rude behavior, clearing out whole categories and then going through the books in a corner, leaving the rejects for someone else to put away, blocking aisles with carts and large boxes, and making the sale atmosphere unpleasant for other shoppers. This is not true of all dealers, and most used booksellers deplore the behavior of the few rude ones. A recent informal survey of dealers provided some suggestions for keeping the sale friendly. Consider your prices; perhaps they are too low. As one dealer put it, "Ten-cent books lead to a smash-and-grab mentality." Prices need to be high enough that dealers must pick and choose carefully.

Posting rules of behavior and then enforcing them, while it may be momentarily unpleasant, is important in controlling the occasional rude patron. (Reputable and courteous dealers applaud when Friends deal firmly with rude patrons.) Dealers appreciate the establishment of a holding area, where they can leave boxes or bags of books while they shop for more. It's wise to stipulate that whatever is left in the holding area is considered purchased, and in fact a volunteer or two can add up the purchases while the books are being held, thus saving time at the checkout. (See **Book sales, etiquette**)

BOOK SALES, DONATION OF BOOKS FOR

 *CD Reference: Book Sales*

Donations from the community often make up the most salable stock at a used-book sale. Both the library and the Friends group need to establish policies in place about receiving book donations, including what donations are acceptable, a review of donations for possible inclusion in the library collection, and reserving the right of the library and Friends to make use of the donated items in whatever way seems best to them. When donations are solicited from the community, there must be a system in place for receiving them, so that people know where to bring their books and when they will be accepted. Newspaper articles and public service announcements can be used to publicize the opportunities for book donation. Some Friends groups distribute flyers at local garage sales and make arrangements with tag sale planners to take leftover books. Offering to pick up large donations of books is helpful. Items other than books that many Friends groups accept include posters and pictures, audio and videotapes, puzzles and games, records, and magazines. Donations that are made to the Friends, who usually accept a wider selection of used and new books than the library would, are usually checked first by the library to see if there are any books that would fill a gap in the collection. If the Friends group has nonprofit status, a donation to it is tax-deductible. (See **Gift policy**)

BOOK SALES, ETIQUETTE

 *CD Reference: Book Sales*

The potent lure of finding a bargain or the perfect gift can cause normally polite library users to forget their manners at a book sale, especially if they have their eye on a favorite book. Add dealers who have wider interests and potentially larger budgets, and there is cause to post a few guidelines that remind customers to mind their manners. (See **Book sales, dealers at**)

BOOK SALES, LEFTOVERS

If a book sale has been well advertised and well attended, and especially if it has ended with a half-price or bag sale or both, there should be very few leftovers that are worth holding over for another sale. Near the end of the sale some of your experienced sorting volunteers can look at what's left, pull out any hidden treasures that deserve another chance, and take note of the sort of books that remain, as that may give you some clues about what to discard and how to price.

Some Friends groups invite not-for-profits that can use books, such as homeless shelters, tutoring programs, and jails, to come during the closing hours and take what they can use. Often it is suggested that the leftovers be boxed up and sent to Africa or Appalachia or some other area in need. Evaluate these suggestions carefully. Books are heavy and expensive to ship out of the country, and many of the leftovers may be so out-of-date as to be a burden to the recipient rather than a welcome gift. A dealer or auctioneer may make you an offer for your leftovers; most groups insist that anyone buying the leftovers must remove all of them.

Some books, sad to say, are ready to be recycled at the end of the sale and need to be taken to the nearest recycler that will accept books. Most Friends groups have found that putting out boxes and mounds of books at the end of the sale for people to take away free simply results in a disorderly mess and actually reduces sales at the end of the sale.

BOOK SALES, MEDIA ATTENTION

Send press releases and public service announcements about the book sale to newspapers and radio stations in your own community and the surrounding area. Be sure to include all the information: days and dates, hours, location. If you have something especially interesting or unusual, include mention of it in your press release, and offer to provide additional information or interviews for feature stories about the sale. Sale preparations often offer interesting photo and video opportunities, so be sure to let the newspapers and television news know what they might be able to picture.

BOOK SALES, MERCHANDISING  *CD Reference: Book Sales*

It is important to make your book sale as appealing as possible without spending large amounts of money, or making it too difficult for volunteers to keep it attractive for the patrons. Much depends on the venue. If shelves are available they can be a big plus, but they may also make it harder to shop from and are harder to keep neat during a big sale. If tables are used, keeping at least thirty-six inches between tables is desirable, more if you have the space. A few boxes of books under the tables may be necessary at a big sale, but try to avoid storing excess stock under tables. Category signs can be printed on ordinary paper, put in plastic page protectors, and stored in a loose-leaf notebook. It's easy to take them to a wall or slide them into a sign holder right in their protectors. Similar book categories placed next to each other make it easier for browsers: psychology next to self-help next to health; thrillers next to mysteries; hobbies and crafts next to sports and games.

During the sale several volunteers need to circulate through the sale, tidying up the tables or shelves, returning books to their proper categories, handing out boxes and bags to customers, and answering questions. Keeping the sale neat is a constant challenge, but the effort is well repaid by a more pleasant atmosphere and easier browsing. These volunteers should have name tags identifying them as Friends, and if your Friends group has its own T-shirts or other distinctive garb they can be encouraged to wear it. Other ways to identify them may include ribbons that say "book sale volunteer," or pins or "straw" hats.

Lining up the books on tables, spine up, with titles all facing the same way, is the time-honored way of displaying books at large sales. Some Friends groups have found it easier to pack their books, spines up, in trimmed-down boxes (soft-drink flats are perfect for paperbacks) and set the boxes on the tables. This eliminates the need for bookends, makes setting up much quicker, and is easier to keep neat. As the flat boxes empty they can be removed and the remaining books consolidated.

Some Friends groups offer a special area for children during the sale, with storytellers, crafts, or cookies. Most find that setting up the children's books in an area separated from the main sale traffic is helpful to parents who are trying to shop with their children.

BOOK SALES, ONLINE AUCTION

When considering selling books on an auction website, be sure to look at the number of items actually receiving bids, and choose a site where there are active bidders. An auction site such as eBay provides a large audience for your items and is a good place to sell unusual, specialized, and celebrity-related items. Selling at auction gives you control over timing, as you can list items at times when volunteers are most available to monitor the e-mail, answer questions, receive payments, and ship items. Auction selling also involves writing an accurate and interesting description of your item and providing a picture, either a digital photograph or a scan. Establish a minimum bid price, and determine what you will ask as shipping fees. The United States Postal Service website, www.usps.com, is very useful for estimating what your mailing expenses might be. Consider also the costs of padded envelopes or other shipping supplies when you set shipping fees. It's necessary to decide how to accept payment from buyers. Many sellers do accept personal checks, but do not ship merchandise until the check clears. It is helpful to be able to accept credit card payments, and there are online payment services, **PayPal** being perhaps the best-known, that will clear credit card payments for a fee. Most auction sites will charge a small listing fee, which you pay even if the item does not sell, and take a percentage of the final sale price as well. (See **Book sales, selling online**)

BOOK SALES, ONLINE FIXED-PRICE

When you list books for sale on a fixed-price website such as Amazon.com, Abebooks.com, Half.com, or Library BookSales.org, you have essentially opened a bookstore and entered into a long-term commitment. Someone will need to check the e-mail daily for questions and for sold notices. Generally an online seller guarantees to ship books within two business days of receiving an order, and most online sellers pride themselves on same-day shipping. Amazon.com is a good venue for selling books that are recent enough to have an International Standard Book Number (ISBN), since your used copy can be listed on the same page where Amazon sells the item new. Amazon does charge a fee but only when the book sells, at which time it collects from the buyer and credits your account. Amazon's "shipping allowance" is a fixed amount, which may or may not cover your actual shipping expenses. On other fixed-price sites, you may be able to set your own shipping fees, and on most of the others you must also arrange payment directly with your buyers. Some sites require a monthly fee, for which you are liable whether or not you have any sales. Conditions change constantly on the Internet; it's well to explore the fees and services on several sites.

A recently established fixed-price listing site is www.librarybooksales.org. It is sponsored by the California State Library and is a selling venue for libraries and library support groups only. There is currently no listing fee and only a 10 percent commission. This site has the potential to become a valuable marketing tool for Friends groups as it grows in numbers of listings and site traffic, and it also provides links to local library sites for browsers who may want to join a local group or donate books.

When you have established an online presence on one or more bookselling sites, be sure to let your local Friends know where they can find those books on the Web. Posting links on your website to your sale listings elsewhere is an excellent idea.

A good resource for anyone entering the online sales field is Stephen Windwalker's *Selling Used Books Online* (Harvard Perspectives, 2002). It's available on Amazon.com or can be ordered directly from the author via his website, http://www.onlinebookselling.net/, which also features news, resources, and helpful links for booksellers. (See **Appendix A; Book sales, selling online**)

BOOK SALES, PREPARATION FOR

In advance of a book sale, the treasurer should get change for the cashboxes. The treasurer needs to devise a system for record keeping, restocking the cashboxes daily, collecting money from the boxes, safeguarding the sale money overnight if necessary, and reporting the income accurately. It's best to appoint one person to remove money from the cashboxes during the sale when they begin to fill up, and to let the cashiers know who that person is. The Friends group needs to have a policy about accepting checks during the sale—whether they will accept checks at all, and if so, whether they will require identification. (Most Friends groups have had no problems accepting checks.)

BOOK SALES, PREVIEWS FOR FRIENDS MEMBERS

A very popular membership perk is a members-only presale held before the book sale opens to the public. The evening before the public sale is one popular time, and some Friends groups have simply reserved the early morning hours of the first day for members only. Members need to receive advance notice and some kind of admission ticket, and volunteers will need to be at the doors to check for proof of membership. Be sure that everyone understands the rules; for instance, how many people may enter on a family membership. Be prepared with extra membership forms and a cashbox so that you can sell Friends memberships at the door during the presale, and be sure to have an up-to-date membership list available to check those who forget to bring their tickets. Friends groups that have members-only presales usually find that it is an effective way to increase their membership. (See **Perks**)

BOOK SALES, PRICING BOOKS

The easiest system for pricing books at a large sale is to establish a base price. Many Friends groups use a base price of one dollar for hardcover books and fifty cents for paperbacks—some have higher base prices and a very few are lower. Establishing a base price allows a great saving of time, energy, and materials that would otherwise be expended in marking prices on every item.

Items that should be priced higher than the base price can be marked by using removable price stickers or by penciling the price lightly on the flyleaf of the book. Consider the convenience of the cashiers when choosing a marking system, as book sale cashiers must often deal with very large stacks of books. It's also important to mark books in a manner that does not destroy their value as possible collector's items, so the use of ink, markers, masking tape, and permanent stickers should be avoided.

Condition and contents should be taken into consideration when pricing individual books. Books in like-new condition (good enough to give as a gift) should be priced higher than the base. General categories of books that may bring prices higher than the base include military topics (especially the Civil War and World War II), specialty cookbooks, books about antiques and collectibles, art books, local histories and other items of special regional interest, and vintage children's books. Taking the time to visit local used-book dealers and check sales prices at online venues will give you a feel for the categories that may need to be specially priced. Most specially priced books will be priced at two or three times the base price, and a few as high as ten times the base. Prices in even dollar amounts are easiest for cashiers to deal with.

If it's possible to hold a multiday sale, it helps to devote a day at the end to a half-price sale and perhaps an additional day to a bag or box sale. This gives possibly overpriced books a chance to find their correct price level, and also helps to clear out the leftovers so that there is less to deal with at the end. Include the special price days in your advertising. Try to make price breaks by day rather than changing in the middle of a day.

Truly valuable books do turn up in book sale donations from time to time. Books autographed by the author, editor, or illustrator should be set aside for special consideration, as should limited editions, books with fine illustrations, county histories and genealogies, and other books that might be of special interest to collectors. First editions of early works by popular authors are often sought after as well. Researching these books online helps book sale volunteers learn to recognize the books that should be given special treatment.

Some Friends groups hold special sales of their more expensive and collectible items, and some establish a separate area of their regular book sale for displaying and selling these books. Perhaps the most common way of dealing with special items at a book sale is by showcasing them in a "silent auction" format, where customers are invited to submit sealed bids and the book is sold to the highest bidder. Items that appear to be valuable but are too specialized to sell well locally may be considered for online selling.

BOOK SALES, PRICING POLICY

A Friends group that sells books needs to have a policy in place about offering (or agreeing to) special prices, as there are always customers who ask about discounts or who want to negotiate prices. It should be clear who in the group, if anyone, has the authority to negotiate. For simplicity's sake, most groups decide that they will not bargain during the book sale.

BOOK SALES, PUBLICITY FOR

One key ingredient in a successful book sale is the buyer-to-book ratio: the more people who come to your sale, the more books you will sell. Information about an upcoming book sale should always be featured in the library's newsletter, the Friends' newsletter, and the library's website. Posters can be distributed throughout the community, with special attention to places such as colleges and universities, coffeehouses, and high-traffic sites such as supermarkets. Bookmarks with the sale hours can be easily produced on plain paper and distributed at the library or included in a mailing.

A good way to reach interested book buyers outside your own community is to list your sale on www.booksalefinder.com. This website reaches many serious book shoppers, and listing is free. Capture drive-by traffic with exterior signs that are large, simple, and eye-catching. A "Book Sale Today" banner on the outside of the library building or similar signs with arrows on nearby corners will bring in people who may have missed or forgotten earlier publicity. One Friends group sponsors a scarecrow contest on the library lawn the same weekend as their fall book sale—anyone coming to see the scarecrows can't miss the book sale.

BOOK SALES, SELLING ONLINE

More and more Friends groups are turning to online sales as a way of supplementing their local sales and finding markets for items that may not sell well locally. Successful online selling requires volunteers with a real interest in learning about bookselling and the time to research, list, pack, and ship books. If such volunteers can be found, online sales can be a valuable addition to your local book sales.

Books can be sold online by auction or on a fixed-price website. It's a good idea to explore several sales venues before making a decision. You will need to register as a seller, which will involve providing information such as a credit card number or bank account number, or perhaps both. If your Friends group does not have its own credit card, a personal card can be used if one of your officers or volunteers is willing. Eventually, however, especially if online sales become a large venture for your group, you'll want to investigate getting a card in the name of the Friends for this purpose. (See **Book sales, online auction; Book sales, online fixed-price; Internet**)

BOOK SALES, SMELLY BOOKS

The dilemma of when you accept donations: to toss a smelly book or try to rejuvenate it. Don't give up on a book too quickly. Try one of these tried and true cures. Put the book in a plastic bag with baking soda or charcoal and seal it. Be careful not to let the book touch any of the product you're using to absorb the odor. Another highly recommended method is time-consuming, so it should probably be done only if the value of the book is high. It is said to take out smoke smells and damp smells: rip black-and-white newspaper into pieces the size of or slightly larger than the pages of the book. Put one piece of newspaper between every page. Leave for at least a week and then remove. Newspaper and newspaper ink are good absorbers of smells. You don't want to leave the newsprint in there forever or the ink could transfer to the paper or the paper could turn brown. Keep for just a few weeks. Repeat if necessary.

BOOK SALES, SORTING FOR

CD Reference: Book Sales

In general, the larger the sale, the more important it is to sort books into categories for easier shopping. The first step in sorting is to discard anything that is musty (the odor will spread and ruin other books), too dirty to clean up, falling apart, or too outdated to sell. Some groups establish a timeline for such items as textbooks. For instance, those less than ten years old go into the sale, those more than fifty years old are also put in the sale as possible collectibles, and those in between are given away or discarded. Reference books and travel guides are other types that need to be culled. It's important to remember that some patrons will be looking for older books, so age alone is not a criterion in most categories. Paperback books with the front covers torn off should not be sold even if otherwise in good condition; such books were likely declared destroyed by a book dealer and should not be in circulation. A small book sale might simply be sorted into fiction and nonfiction, but once a sale grows to more than eight tables of books, you will want to establish more specific categories to help your customers find what they want.

BOOK SALES, VOLUNTEERS

A used-book sale requires lots of time and energy, so it's crucial to develop a good strong volunteer pool. Some jobs require a consistent year-round commitment, such as sorting books. Others are perfect opportunities for the Friends member who can donate only a few hours a year and who may be happy to come and be a cashier for two or three hours. You can ask on your membership form if the member would like to be called to help with book sales; be sure that everyone who offers does get a phone call. As with all volunteer tasks, making the job fun and friendly is vital. Volunteers need clear instructions, name tags, introductions to other volunteers, coffee and cookies, and a sense that what they are doing is making a difference. Thank-you notes are especially effective when they mention how much money was raised. One Friends group sends all of its volunteers an e-mail update every evening during the sale as soon as the day's money has been counted. **Volunteers** who have a good time and feel that the project was worth their time will want to participate again. Making all volunteers feel part of the team really pays off.

For the heaviest tasks involving strong backs, such as moving the boxes of books to the sale area and setting up and taking down tables, consider recruiting a group such as a service club, a youth group or Scout troop, a fraternity or sorority, or a high school athletic team. Many groups welcome the opportunity for community service and will be glad to come and help for a specific task. Work carefully with the adult sponsors of youth groups to be sure that there will be adequate chaperonage and supervision from the group itself.

BOOKMARKS

The omnipresent bookmark is vastly underrated as means of marketing the Friends. At the very least one should be available for every book checked out of the library with the Friends' name emblazoned on it, contact information, and their logo. It can also carry a short membership form, enabling the user to send in money to the right address. It can carry messages about forthcoming programs or book sales. Some libraries hold contests and have winning pictures done by schoolchildren copied on them. Some ask community artists to enter a competition, and the winning entry is copied on it, and a raffle is held for the original artwork. Bookmarks should be available at book sales and at library checkout desks. (See **Publications**)

BOOKSTORES

Both small independent bookstores and large national chains such as Borders and Barnes & Noble can be happy partners for Friends groups in many ways. It is best to work with them, rather than regard them as competition. Bookstores are able to partner with a Friends group by giving discounts to members, perhaps for a limited number of times a year; they can also handle large orders of books for special programs and provide help with selling and shipping them back to the publisher. They can cosponsor programs that will enhance your audience, and many times will have promotional items that your members may enjoy. Most Friends buy books as well as borrow them from the library, so it is always good business for a bookstore to show that it regards them as important customers.

BRANCH FRIENDS

CD Reference: Running a Board

Branch libraries have devoted patrons who use their library and may seldom have need for the central library. Because branch libraries serve a specific neighborhood, they are likely to have less diverse demographics than a citywide group. They can make the basis for a loyal group of Friends, whose interests do not extend beyond their neighborhood as far as libraries go. Friends groups that serve branch libraries generally duplicate the activities of a larger group, albeit on a smaller, more personal scale. Depending on the population of the area, they may be more interested in children's programs, or senior programs, crafts, etc. They may have a bake sale or rummage sale in connection with a book sale. Their meetings may involve their local politician speaking about a specific area problem. They may ally with a central group for certain activities, but are most comfortable in raising money for their branch. In a system with many branches, groups often support an umbrella Friends group. The umbrella group sees the branch Friends as important advocacy partners and may handle much of the paperwork for the branches, such as filing IRS returns, keeping up with state requirements, etc. Because of the neighborhood orientation, these groups may have more ethnic influences than the central group, and may use their funds to buy special materials, or celebrate different holidays. It is not uncommon for the central group to make gifts to those groups from neighborhoods with fewer financial resources. (See **Citywide Friends**)

BROCHURES   *CD Reference: Publications*

Brochures are necessary to acquaint the public with your Friends organization. A brochure can be only a single piece of paper, but take care to make it attractive, not too cluttered, and concise. Getting people interested is most important: details may be given in another way. To identify the Friends as separate from the library, a name should be chosen ("Friends of Such-and-such Library" is easy), and a distinctive **logo**. At the beginning you may want to hold a contest for a logo, or ask for professional help—pro bono, of course. Dues should be listed, your mission statement, and program plans if they exist. A contact number and an address to mail dues to are necessary. If the brochure doubles as a return-by-mail form, be sure to leave room for an address label to be affixed. Brochures should be available at the library and at other community events and places that the public would see them. Other brochures can discuss other opportunities, for volunteers, for book sale help, for donations of different sorts. Be sure that each brochure is different in some way, so that they are not discarded because they seem to be duplicates. (See **Publications**)

BUDGETS   *CD Reference: Running a Board*

A budget lists the anticipated income and expenses for the fiscal year of an organization. It is made up with input from the various committees and from past experience, and usually incorporates a slight increase based on hopes for a successful year. A budget is a management tool that reflects your goals as a Friends organization. It is also a public document, one that your board of directors must approve. The **treasurer** is responsible for budget oversight. A budget must be regarded as flexible, since elements of it are hard to predict, and it may have to be adjusted during the **fiscal year.** This means that when expenses get too high, items in the budget have to be cut; if donations are generous, you may have the opportunity to spend more than planned. Typical budget items are as follows:

> Income: dues, donations, sales (tickets, book or gift sales), grants, interest, and other fund-raising projects. Depending on how you bill your memberships, you may have income coming in all year round if you bill members each year in the month they joined, or all at once if all memberships start at the beginning of your fiscal year.

> Expenses: newsletter (postage, paper, printing), membership (postage, printing, stationery), meeting costs, salary if there are employees (in which case you would have federal, state, and local taxes to consider), office equipment, rentals, and upkeep, library donations, rent, refreshments, board expenses, program expenses, telephone, Internet connection, computer hardware and software, etc. For a small Friends group, most of these expenses would be donated, and office expenses would be minimal if done at home by volunteers. There is a good chance the library would be willing to let its space and some supplies or phones be used if they are available. Having a donor who will help buffer the beginning expenses can be a tremendous help.

The factors involved in planning a budget are almost all variable, which is why the budget is so important. If your group is spending more than it is making, it is not healthy, as in any other business. The budget should be discussed at your monthly board meetings to keep it under control and to see if a push is needed in membership or help is needed in another area, such as cutting expenses.

Budgets can take many different forms, but all are necessary. The first budget for a new Friends organization is usually pure guesswork, and must be adjusted to fit the reality of the situation. Those first heady days when ideas and possibilities seem eminently doable eventually face reality. Finding resources and forging partnerships in the community can stretch a budget, but there are some expenses that always have to be dealt with. Finding out what financial help the library is prepared to undertake would be the first step, and finding out what the Friends officers need to carry out their duties is the second. Very often start-up costs for the initial period are underwritten, sometimes with the library's help, with due credit given. Mailing and printing costs may comprise the largest part of the budget, assuming that everything else is volunteered. A bulk mail permit is an option if you send out 500 or more pieces of mail at a time. Using the library's mail permit, or attaching the Friends' mailings to the library's mailings, are other ways to avoid the expense. In some communities, the gas or electric utilities will help with the mailings. Learning what to charge for dues and for programs is an important part of making the group viable. Learning who to ask for help makes up the second part of that equation. Planning a budget is an ongoing process with many factors to be taken into consideration, the primary one being to help the library as much as possible. This may be through cash donations for special purposes, raising public awareness, and advocacy and volunteer efforts. All these have an impact on the budget.

BULK MAIL

Getting a bulk mail permit for the Friends organization really depends on the size and frequency of your mailings. If your group sends out 500 or more pieces of mail at a time, a bulk mail permit is an option. Once there is an idea of what mailings will be made, and how many addresses will receive them, discuss the options with your local postmaster. If prompt delivery of your mailings is important, it is possible that bulk mail would not be efficient. For excellent information about mailing choices, go to the United States Postal Service website and choose "Business Mail 101": http://www.usps.com/businessmail101/.

BUSINESS PARTNERS: see **Partners, business.**

BYLAWS

CD Reference: Legal Necessities

A Friends organization generally has two documents that govern it: the bylaws and the constitution. Of the two, the bylaws are the more specific. While the constitution might mention a board of directors, the bylaws will specify a board of no less than ten members or more than twenty. The constitution will say that officers will govern the organization, and the bylaws will say the officers will be a president, vice president, secretary, and treasurer. It is best not to be too specific even in the bylaws, which need to be voted on by the group's entire membership when adopted and if changed. For instance, saying what the specific board positions are is not wise; they can change with each year, since some evolution in activities is normal. What has to be made clear in the bylaws is who can vote on the board, who votes to elect the board, and that upon dissolution of the organization, any monies remaining will go to the library, since the organization is formed to benefit the library. It is important to assure how a position on the board is filled if someone has to vacate their spot prematurely. It is also important to stipulate the length of the terms of office each board member may serve.

CAPITAL CAMPAIGNS

A Friends group will undertake a capital campaign whenever a library needs a major improvement. The improvement is usually bricks and mortar, but in recent years capital campaigns have also raised funds for technological and public accessibility improvements. Once the need for an improvement is recognized by the library trustees or the director, it is necessary to see how the people in control of the public purse strings feel about the issue. If funding is available from federal or state sources, if local tax money is available, and if a referendum may be held are all factors that determine how much public money is possible. A capital campaign is the public part of an effort that has started years before. Major gifts are solicited quietly, so that once there is a public campaign they can be announced. This all takes a great deal of time. Development specialists are generally hired for a capital campaign. Friends are not usually involved in the planning unless they play a large financial role in the library. They are most necessary in the public part of the campaign, when their lists of contacts must be individually reached and told the importance of the project. The Friends may form a speakers' bureau to go to other community organizations to speak about the project. Friends will also be called upon to help with the celebration once the project is finished. It is useful to have the Friends group organized prior to a project like this, because if formed for the project itself, the group may feel without a purpose once it is finished. (See **Issue statement**)

CAUSE-RELATED MARKETING

This type of marketing connects a worthy cause (the library Friends) with a for-profit business that wants to benefit from a public affiliation with the

Friends (and the library). In return, the Friends group receives monetary contributions or services from the business. For example, a local restaurant might offer a discount to Friends members on a certain date; a bank or supermarket could encourage customers to drop off books for the book sale and deliver them to the library; or a store might give a percentage of its receipts for one day to the library. It's up to the Friends to set a policy about the desirability of such efforts. This type of arrangement may lead to publicity and money, or it may create more work than profit. Some Friends groups have developed guidelines about the types of businesses they will deal with; for instance, a group might want to exclude dealings with a company advertising alcohol or tobacco products. (The business point of view on this topic is given at www.crm.org.uk.) Interestingly, businesses do not always want their names used in these ventures, although they are willing to help in some way. They are protecting themselves from being asked to aid other causes. (See **Corporate support; Partners, business**)

CENTER FOR THE BOOK

This organization was established in 1977 to use the resources and prestige of the Library of Congress (LC) to promote books, reading, libraries, and literacy. Within the LC, the Center is a focal point for celebrating the legacy of books and the printed word. Outside the LC, the Center works closely with other organizations to foster understanding of the vital role of books, reading, libraries, and literacy in society. On behalf of books and reading, the Center for the Book serves as an advocate, a catalyst, and a source of ideas—both nationally and internationally. The national group has chapters in each state, and these groups provide an excellent resource for Friends. These groups can become partners in various Friends activities, and they are especially involved in Literary Landmark programs. Making an overture to a state chapter for an informal liaison would be helpful, and you can locate them on the Web by going to the main website at http://lcweb.loc.gov/loc/cfbook/ and looking up state Center affiliates.

CHARTER MEMBERS

When a Friends group is started, it may call the original members "charter members" and give them some honor, such as having their names displayed on a plaque in the library, or inviting them to a special reception at someone's home. An announcement should be made with a cutoff date for becoming a charter member. There may also be a special one-time dues level for them.

CITYWIDE FRIENDS *CD Reference: Running a Board*

A city library that has one very successful Friends group and a number of branch libraries with and without their own Friends groups can be the breeding ground for a larger effort. This would keep the central Friends group intact but adds the ability to organize Friends at branches without them as part of the central group's mission. The branches would have the advantage of not having to start from scratch, since they could come under the existing main organization's 501(c)(3) nonprofit status and file a tax return if necessary through their affiliation with the main organization as an added benefit. A central constitution and bylaws for the citywide group would determine the obligations of both groups. Officers and a board of directors would be chosen from all libraries for the parent group, and a small board chosen for each branch as well. These branch groups are especially useful for advocacy purposes, and do not generally have the same activities as the central library Friends. It is not necessary for the smaller groups to meet together more than a few times a year, perhaps when giving out awards to local politicians or to donors and volunteers. Those branches having preexisting Friends are included as part of the network. (See **Branch Friends**)

CODES OF CONDUCT *CD Reference: Policy Manuals*

Confusion about the respective roles played by the Friends board of directors, the library **trustees,** and the library director often leads to conflicts that poison what should be a collegial atmosphere. (See **Control**) While the three entities may not always agree, they should communicate and maintain a high level of congenial behavior. Having representatives of the trustees and Friends attend the other's board meetings is helpful, and provides the means to keep current on library affairs and needs. Assuming that the Friends have their own tax exemption, their decisions on how their money will be spent can be informed by hearing from the trustees about the library's current financial state, the needs of various departments, and the programs that will or will not be funded. The library director or his or her representative can also pass on suggestions to the board from various staff members. It is important not to let board members' pet projects influence library management decisions ("every library should have the complete works of Dickens, Hardy, and Henry James on the shelves"). Certainly, the Friends are citizens and should be able to voice their opinions, but only as individuals, not as members of the board. The board should have a single voice, and be supportive of the library. This is usually not a problem, but it can become one if there are difficult personalities on either board. The trustees do not "run" the Friends, and both boards support the library. The **Successful Friends Policy** has proven useful in delineating their respective roles.

COFFEE SHOPS

The Friends can underwrite a coffee shop in the library with minimal involvement, if they so wish, or they can make it a major project that is handled by volunteers. It is now accepted in many libraries that patrons enjoy the ability to buy a cup of coffee or tea, and perhaps other beverages and snacks. An arrangement can be made with a local purveyor to bring in large thermos containers of the beverages and hot water, and to replace them during the day. A volunteer can take the money, or if there are no objections, a librarian. This can be a simple operation on a table, or a special cart can be set up in the lobby and moved out of the way when not in use. The coffee shop provides a good opportunity to speak to patrons and involve them in the Friends.

COMMITMENT

Be aware and appreciate that members of the Friends have made a level of commitment by joining. There are many levels of commitment to the Friends, stemming from many motives for affiliation. For someone to be a dues-paying member of the Friends is the lowest level, perhaps, but necessary for the group to exist. These members recognize the importance of the library and its support group and give money as a civic duty. They may never attend a program or a book sale. Others members may join to meet others with similar interests. (See **Membership**) The next level would be to attend those events, and eventually to volunteer to help if asked. Agreeing to serve on a committee for an event leads to meeting more of the group than at previous stages, and if the climate is found suitable, if the group is welcoming, these people may agree to serve on the board of directors if asked. By joining the board they have made a large commitment of time and energy. Not only will they be expected to attend meetings, but also to attend events when possible. Becoming the chair of a committee is a further responsibility. Becoming an officer is the greatest commitment (except for vice presidents in most organizations). When you think of the extra hours given by the secretary, treasurer, and president, it is a reminder of how important each individual is to the strength of the group as a whole.

COMMITTEES

The committees in a Friends group are meant to carry out the work of the board of directors. Their members can be board members as well as ordinary members of the Friends. It is necessary to make sure that every committee has a real function, and that each board member participates in at least one committee. There may be permanent committees, such as ones for nominating, membership, program, book sale, fund-raising, etc.; and temporary committees that are set up for a special purpose, such as a special event. Each committee must have a chair who is responsible for calling meetings at appropriate intervals, at a time convenient for most members on the committee. The chair reports on the committee's actions at the board meeting. The president of the board is usually a de facto member of any committee and can attend or not, or ask the vice president to attend. In the case of the **nominating committee,** it is helpful for the full board to offer suggestions during the year, and the nominating committee takes them under advisement with due consideration of the terms and makeup of the existing board. Committees may meet at the library or at a member's home. A new Friends organization is usually started by the **steering committee,** which disbands following the election of the first board. Most boards also make allowances for emergency meetings by selecting an **executive committee,** comprised of officers and committee chairs.

COMMUNITY INVOLVEMENT

The Friends are part of a larger community and necessarily have contacts with other groups in it. This is especially important when the Friends are having a membership drive, or when the library needs advocacy support to contact local politicians. An informal speakers' bureau already exists, with the local Friends members reaching out to their circles of acquaintances; it just has to be put into action. When there is a major issue regarding the library (see **Advocacy; Capital campaigns**), ask the attendees of a general program as well as board members what other organizations they belong to. Make a list on a large poster. Explain to them what the issue is and why you are asking for their help, noting the wide spread of influence in the room. Ask them to take issue statements that have been prepared and use them as talking points the next time they attend another group's meeting. It is amazing how many people can be reached in this way. (See **Issue statement**)

Community involvement also involves the Friends group itself. Friends should be represented at meetings of local nonprofit organizations, if they exist. Each nonprofit group can learn from another; take advantage of each other to bolster audiences and to recruit new members; buy supplies in quantity to save money; participate in citywide celebrations; and raise the group's profile. The Friends should participate in or attend local government meetings, make media contacts for special events, and send representatives to other groups to involve them in special events. Women's Clubs have historic ties to libraries and literacy, and PTAs and PTOs can be vital allies in causes involving children. Rotary clubs and chambers of commerce can be valuable allies as well. Check with the library director for ideas about reaching out to other groups, and ask spouses and friends for ideas.

CONSTITUTION

The constitution is the preeminent document of a Friends organization. Once written it is generally not modified, barring extraordinary circumstances. The constitution generally begins with the **mission statement**. (See **Annual meeting; Bylaws; Nonprofit status**)

CONTRACTS   *CD Reference: Running a Board*

It can make the business of the board of directors much easier if there are contracts to back up decisions on hiring and firing, as well as contracts for rentals, catering, space, and equipment. There should be a contract for employees hired by the board, and there should also be one for volunteers, so they know what is expected of them. A contract helps ensure that both sides understand expectations. It is also useful to have a type of understanding for the board itself, so members know what is expected of them as well. It is wise to let an attorney on the board look over the contracts to make sure there are no hidden loopholes. An overlooked or misunderstood phrase in a contract can come back to haunt the group.

CONTROL

Libraries foster two groups, the **trustees** and the Friends, both of which want the best for their library. However, tensions over roles and control typically occur between the Friends and the trustees or the Friends and the library director or a member of the library staff. Conflict is usually related to how to spend the funds that the Friends raise. If the Friends have their own 501(c)(3) status they can decide how to spend this money, but they owe it to the library to work with the director. If the director submits a wish list, it can ease the tension. The trustees work with the library director and should have a joint liaison situation with the Friends, but the trustees do not control the Friends' actions. If the Friends do not have a separate tax ID, then their money may disappear into the library's or community's general budget, and the Friends' raison d'etre is lost. When the cause of tension is personal, the Friends have to realize that not all library staff like having Friends around and may feel that their turf is threatened, or it may truly be a personality conflict. In either case, that staff member should be given space and another way found to accomplish the task. (See **Codes of conduct**)

CORPORATE SUPPORT

A lifeline to many Friends groups is available from the willing hands of various businesses in the community that will help out when needed. Corporate support is not completely altruistic; business is business, and recognition of their help is mandatory. The goodwill that a library is privy to is very important in making contacts, and in taking advantage of the contacts of board members and others in the Friends group. Businesses of all types can provide prizes for events; services such as printing, mailing, design, and publicity; and most important, a fertile group of potential new board members. One of the most popular fund-raisers of recent years involved gift baskets donated by businesses and volunteer groups, to be auctioned off to benefit the library. Without good partners, it would be difficult to do this type of fund-raising. (See **Cause-related marketing; Partners, business**)

CORRESPONDENCE   *CD Reference: Donations and Membership*

Some Friends groups may have a separate position for a corresponding secretary who handles official letters for the group. However, most groups divide this labor among the committee heads. If there is no official stationery, there should at least be note cards with the Friends group's name on it, perhaps with a stamp or sticker. If there is letterhead available, it should have the group's official EIN number listed on it. Thank-you notes for donations should carry that information as well.

CRAFT PROJECTS

Mothers attending Friends meetings at the library often have to bring their children along, sometimes at the last minute. It is not good form to expect the librarians to entertain the children while the group meets. Depending on how often this situation occurs at your library, the Friends should provide a box for this purpose only, containing some craft materials and toys that will keep young children occupied. The craft materials can be simple, perhaps paper in different colors, crayons or markers (be careful not to let children armed with art supplies migrate near library books!), stickers, tape, and other nondisruptive materials. These should be used for emergencies only. (See **Appendix A**)

DEMOGRAPHICS

Demographics is the study of population—both its characteristics and the geography where that population lives. Your community's demographics are important to know so that you can market your Friends memberships appropriately to specific groups. The chief characteristics of a population are its age, race or ethnicity, income, language, education, and religious affiliations. Every community is made up of smaller communities, and they are all the target audience of the library and of the Friends. (See **Diversity**)

DEVELOPMENT OFFICE

A development office helps to find alternative funding through grants and large donations to the library as a whole, or to specific departments within it, depending on the donor's wishes. Both academic and public libraries may have development offices, but usually it is only the largest libraries that do. In academic institutions, the college or university has its own development office, which may not work closely with the library, or may generally include it in their giving options. There is an ongoing educational campaign among academic librarians to increase their libraries' visibility to donors to the institution; Friends play a big role in this. Since the library serves all students, not just graduates, but all those who just attended the school without graduating, the library can attract donors who might not feel attached to a particular school. The development office can help the library and the Friends by sharing its resources for keeping records, doing large mailings, and sharing information. In a public library, the development office can partner with the Friends to develop larger events, provide support to include a larger base for mailings, provide materials for the Friends to use in their solicitations, and approach those major donors who may not be comfortable working with a volunteer group. It is very important for the Friends and the development office to coordinate the prospects they solicit for funds, and these relationships become even more complicated with the presence of a library foundation. (See **Academic Friends; Foundations**)

DIRECTOR, LIBRARY: see **Library director.**

DIRECTORS, BOARD OF: see **Board of directors.**

DIVERSITY   *CD Reference: Running a Board*

It is important that the Friends identify the various groups that make up their community (see **Demographics**) and represent these groups on their board. Avoid having boards populated by members who are all over fifty years old, or who are all stay-at-home moms. Library directors can help point out patrons from the community who might be interested in serving on the board. Some immigrant populations may not yet have the necessary language skills to participate, but their high schoolers might, and can have a special place on the board. New immigrant communities may not be aware of the strong volunteer culture in the United States; it may not have been part of their tradition. It is important to convey to them how important citizen involvement is to the life of the community. It is possible to discuss this with their community leaders and clergy, who could also represent them on the board. The Friends and the library can reach them by supporting library programming that highlights the various cultures and skills (music, celebrations, dance, crafts, storytelling) in the community. Some

Friends groups have had success by offering to finance special collections in different languages.

There should be a sliding scale of dues for members so that no one is left out. Senior members on limited budgets may not feel included, but this waning World War II generation has a lot to teach those young members who are struggling for the first time to make ends meet. Their recollections and tips can be the basis for a local publication or cookbook about coping when times are tough, or for a local column under the Friends name in the library newsletter. They can also be a fund of knowledge for retiring baby boomers who may have a new interest in knitting, quilting, sewing, or any number of craft techniques that were briefly out of style, bringing in new members to the Friends.

Offering walking tours of the community or tours of the library or cemeteries or other historic places can be done by a committee of volunteers who are willing to train themselves by studying the local records and making them into a narrative. Finding out stories of eccentric former residents adds to the mix. Sometimes local colleges are willing to aid in these efforts, which can result in special publications. A special event highlighting the various ethnic communities, a miniature folk fair, with tastes of different ethnic food specialties, demonstrations of crafts, and music and dance is a delight for spectators and participants. If the Friends group has enough warning, it may be able to gather enough patches to assemble into a quilt to be raffled off for the library, reflecting the variety of the event. (See **Maintenance; Programs**)

DOCUMENT STORAGE

There are any number of documents that should be stored in order to have a record of the Friends group's activities. Certain documents must be kept by law. Keeping a balance between too many and too few documents is a problem, not only for storage purposes but for the records themselves. (See **Record keeping**) Too often records are kept, with the best intentions, by board members who have space available in their homes. They are eventually forgotten there, get lost, and disappear. If your group is technically adept, or if the librarian is willing to help, many of your records can be kept on CD-ROM disks or other technology that will not be a space issue. These records should be kept at the library once the fiscal year is over. They should include minutes, treasurer's reports, audits, IRS returns, the group's mission statement, constitution, and bylaws, any significant agreements, and copies of minutes of the annual meeting. A hard-copy file of the group's newsletters is always a good idea, since photos are usually greatly enjoyed after the group has celebrated enough anniversaries to make the photos seem historical. Other special paper documents can be kept in a file, such as special publications, programs, examples of special outreach programs, and photos of the group working on projects like book sales. Each committee should also keep a record book that can be passed on to the next chair. Subtle changes may occur in a Friends group each year, and in a matter of five years or so the changes may be significant. These records make it possible for the group's members to assess if they are pleased with the way the group is going, or if the mission has shifted. Some of the group's financial records may be kept by the **treasurer** if that position is a long-term one, but there should always be duplicate copies in the library. If the group has an accountant, his or her office may keep some of the records, but the Friends should have a copy in their own library space. The Friends should ask the library if it will provide a file, or pay for one, in which to keep their records.

DONATIONS

CD Reference: Donations and Membership

Donations can take many forms. There are donations of time from your members. There are donations of books. There are monetary donations, gifts, and dues, on which the Friends group depends. Then there are many gifts-in-kind donations; these are just as important as tangible gifts, and must always be acknowledged. (See **Awards; Recognition**) These can be the gifts of self from board members or volunteers, special skills that they share with you. They can be marketing techniques for membership or fundraising, accounting support, legal advice or support, help with publications (including layout and design), printing, paper, free promotion, donations of goods that can be used for promotion, entertainment, catering, and space to hold special events. These services may be donated, or made available at special prices. They can come from large corporations or small local businesses. They can be as large as a car for a raffle, or as small as some hamburgers or pizzas.

Once the board is made aware of the needs of the Friends group, its members can begin to look among their friends and acquaintances for appropriate help. Sometimes this is the only function of a board member with no personal time to spare but lots of contacts. The library director also has many contacts, but may find it easier for the Friends to do the asking. If you watch the PBS stations' fund-raising campaigns, you hear them thanking all sorts of businesses for support. Libraries certainly serve an even wider audience than do these stations. In a survey of 4,000 adults, the Independent Sector (http://www.independentsector.org/programs/research/gv01main.html) found that 89 percent of them contribute to charitable organizations, and that the average annual contribution is $1,620. (See **Appendix A; Book sales, donations of books for; Corporate support; Endowments; Gift policy**)

DUE DILIGENCE

Due diligence is a process of investigation, performed by investors, into the details of a potential investment. This term is most often used for the investigations made by major investment concerns, but even a small Friends group's use of the money it collects must also be considered an investment. It is necessary for Friends to consider their expenditures with due diligence. Sometimes there are board members who recommend the purchase of items that are useful in their own businesses; this can be very helpful, but it is necessary to check to see if the cost is warranted and the item really is needed by a Friends group. This is fairly easy to do, either by calling other similar groups and finding out what they use, or going on the FOLUSA discussion list and asking for opinions. When purchasing equipment or software, first ask others who use it about their experiences with it. It is other people's money that you are spending and there are many uses for it, but it ultimately must benefit the library. Due diligence is part of being committed to **best practices**.

DUES

There are no established criteria for setting a Friends group's membership dues, except that there has to be a variety of choices to appeal to all segments of the community. Compare the dues asked by other community membership organizations that charge a wide range of fees and then decide where your Friends group fits in. You must assume that some of the public will give a larger amount because they appreciate the worth of the library to the community, and others will appreciate you but can only afford a small amount. It is important to recognize that seniors, heads of large families, and all income groups should be able to find appropriate membership dues. Have several higher levels of dues listed; if someone is able to give more, they will. Members of the board must all be members, at some level, of the organization. (See **Membership**)

EIN NUMBER

CD Reference: Legal Necessities

The EIN number is the Employer Identification Number issued by the Internal Revenue Service to nonprofit organizations, even if they do not have any employees. It is the number the organization uses when asked for proof of its nonprofit status. The number is important to have available for donors who must use it in their records. (See **Incorporation; Nonprofit status; Tax exemption**)

ELECTIONS

Members of the board of directors are elected by the members of a Friends group at regularly scheduled elections, once a year. (See **Annual meeting; Nominating committee**) These have to be publicly announced meetings, giving ample notice as defined in the bylaws and with a quorum present. Each member of the board is elected for a term of office as specified on the ballot (e.g., president for a one-year term; board member for a two-year term). However, it is best to have the board members serve alternate terms, so there are always experienced members on the board, mixed with new members. Members may also serve more than one term on the board, and this should be stipulated in the bylaws. Another common stipulation is that "No member of the Board may serve more than two consecutive terms on the Board of Directors." Board members may, however, serve on committees, as can other members of the Friends who are not on the board. Elections are not a big draw, so they are usually included within an annual program that will be interesting to a good-sized audience.

EMBEZZLING

Bad things can happen to good organizations, and they have. It is necessary to remember that the money donated to the Friends group is a public trust, and there should be safeguards in place to be sure it is carefully used. (See **Audit; Executive director; Fiscal policy**) A member of the board with training should oversee the group's financial details and the check register on an irregular basis, making sure they correlate with the membership records. It is wise to have a system in place stipulating that no check larger than an agreed-upon amount can be cashed without the cosignature of another officer. There should also be a way of making sure that all timely documents—bills as well as legal correspondence from the city, state, or federal governments—are handled in a timely manner.

ENDOWMENTS

An endowment fund is money that has been placed in trust for the library, or for the Friends group, usually for a specific purpose, or for unforeseen emergencies. Often Friends groups start an endowment in anticipation of specific contributions as part of a building project. It is hard for a new group to start an endowment fund without a major grant from a benefactor. Money can be added to an endowment fund for a specific purpose by the Friends if they care to make donations to the library foundation, if one exists. Depending on how an endowment was set up, removing funds from it may require special arrangements. The interest from the endowment fund may be reinvested or used toward a specified purpose, or in some cases it may be at the discretion of the library director or trustees. A trusted banker or trust manager is an important advisor for an endowment fund. Many communities have community-run foundations where the library's money is kept for it but is invested as part of the group. Foundations are not a project that many people find exciting, but they can play a decisive role as an option when discussing planned giving with a donor. Many donors will remember the library when disbursing their assets or writing a will. It is wise to check state and local legal requirements before becoming too involved in this type of project. (See **Foundations**)

EVALUATION OF PROGRAMS   *CD Reference: Programs*

All of a group's programs should be evaluated following the event, whether they are long-standing or one-time special events. Changes from the previous year should be noted in suppliers, media coverage, site used, and board involvement. Note if the audiences remain enthusiastic, or become static, or diminish, or there are other signs of stagnation. As different chairs examine a group's programs they bring new perspectives. On the other hand, they may find an unexpectedly successful program that deserves another airing. It is necessary to decide if the goals for the program were met, if the amount of time and the expense put into the project were worth it, or if that portion of the budget could have been better used on another effort. (See **Positioning; Programs**)

EXECUTIVE COMMITTEE

The executive committee is usually comprised of officers, and sometimes committee chairs from the larger board of directors. It may sometimes be referred to as the "executive board," depending on popular usage. This committee must be able to assemble rapidly and to handle sensitive issues. It reports back to the full board. The board may give the committee the power to make decisions on specific issues on behalf of the full board. The committee may also meet between board meetings to discuss issues for which there is no time available at the larger board meetings and bring the discussion back to the board. By doing this it may help make the full board meetings more efficient, especially if they have been running too long.

EXECUTIVE DIRECTOR   *CD Reference: Running a Board*

When a Friends group reaches a certain level of activity, part-time administrative help is no longer an option, and a higher level of support is needed. The term "executive director" is sometimes used for this function, or "executive secretary," or however the group wants to designate the position. It entails a higher level of responsibility for the day-to-day functioning of the group than is expected from an administrative assistant. (See **Office support**) This could include overseeing a bookstore, volunteer recruitment, check writing and money management, membership renewals and tracking, responsibility for board meeting and program planning, keeping track of committee functioning, and carrying out board assignments and programs. This can be a position of great responsibility, and **due diligence** should be taken in the hiring process. If your group is not comfortable with the hiring process, ask the library's human resources department for information, or one of your board members with access to such a department.

EXEMPTION, TAX: see **Tax exemption.**

FINANCES

The finances of a Friends organization come under the jurisdiction of the **treasurer.** The accountant used may be a board member, or an acquaintance of someone on the board. The treasurer should oversee the accountant to make sure that all filings are done on time, and that the group's books are being kept accurately. If the treasurer delegates the group's filings to the accountant (instead of doing them himself), the treasurer should check up on the accountant and be sure that all the necessary files were made available to him. If an employee is in charge of finances, there should be someone to oversee that person, and a compensation or personnel committee should do an annual review. Using the library's tax exemption number may be possible, in order to receive charitable donations and tax exemption from various state and local laws, but doing so may lead to complications about the use of funds collected by the Friends. The point of having these various controls is to make sure that the board is being fiscally responsible and that the group's income covers the expenses of the organization. (See **Accounting; Budgets**)

FINANCIAL DISCLOSURE

On April 8, 1999, the IRS issued T.D. 8818, amending the regulations implementing Section 6104 of the Internal Revenue Code. The amendments generally require tax-exempt organizations (other than private foundations) to provide copies of certain tax documents to requesting individuals; these tax documents are usually to be provided immediately in the case of in-person requests and within thirty days in the case of written requests. The tax-exempt organization may charge a reasonable copying fee plus actual postage, if any. These new disclosure requirements are in addition to the requirement that tax-exempt organizations must make their tax documents available for public inspection.

FISCAL POLICY

Friends groups should have a conservative fiscal policy. This generally means that they work with the money they have in hand from dues, sales, and donations. Their money is invested conservatively. All large expenditures over a set amount (to be set by the board) would require the permission of two board members before they could be spent. It is important to have the group's check-signing card kept up to date with the current president and treasurer's signature on it. In case of them both being out of town, a library staff member might also cosign. Many banks do not send the canceled checks back anymore without charging a slight fee. It is worth paying this fee as an additional safety measure. (See **Bank accounts; Budgets**)

FISCAL YEAR

The year span that is chosen by the board to use to keep the account books is the fiscal year. It does not have to begin the month the group was formed; the first year can be "short." The year can be a calendar year, January through December, or September through August, or any twelve-month period that works for your group. It may make sense as far as annual budget planning goes to have the Friends' budget year begin after the library budget has been announced. This would allow for planning yearly goals more precisely.

FLOWCHART *CD Reference: Programs*

When planning the Friends group's year, or the details of a large undertaking such as a social event or book sale, it helps to let everyone know what is expected of them, when they should be free, and how much time they have to finish their task. A flowchart will break down the work into a schematic drawing that will make it easier for everyone to see their part in the effort, how it affects others, and how to allocate their time. It will also help to plan the event, since all of the tasks have to be recognized and written down.

FOLUSA: see **Friends of Libraries U.S.A.**

FOUNDATIONS *CD Reference: Donations and Membership*

In libraries where there is both a library foundation and a Friends group, there has to be a clear delineation of territory where each group may solicit donations. Many foundations have a long-standing tradition and hold old bequests that have been accruing interest and dividends for decades. This may be in the form of an endowment. Others are of recent origin, when the stock market was riding high and new money gave rise to new largesse. By contrast, most of the Friends' donations come from membership dues and small businesses, as well as community leaders giving gifts to help underwrite special projects or events. In some communities the Friends are the foundation. It takes a large, well-organized Friends group to go after major donations, and this is where conflicts with the foundation can arise. There should be frank and open discussions about which donor is in the purview of the Friends and which is in that of the foundation, so as not to confuse, disrupt, or disturb the donor community. Sometimes the Friends have a special relationship with a donor that it would be meaningless to destroy for the sake of upholding the foundation's purview; careful thought has to be given to any such change. (See **Development office; Endowments**)

FRIENDS OF LIBRARIES U.S.A. (FOLUSA)

Friends of Libraries U.S.A. (FOLUSA) is a national nonprofit organization that provides networking opportunities and educational support for local Friends of Libraries groups across the country. Over 2,000 Friends groups, libraries, and individuals belong to FOLUSA, representing hundreds of thousands of library supporters. Beginning in 1975 as a committee of the Library Administration and Management Association of the American Library Association, it became an independent nonprofit organization in 1979. FOLUSA is now a national leader in library support and advocacy.

Through publications, online resources, training, and support, FOLUSA works with local and state Friends groups to enhance their efforts as advocates, volunteers, program and community outreach catalysts, and as fund-raisers in support of their public and academic libraries.

Since 1989 FOLUSA has annually presented a Public Service Award as part of Library Legislative Day in Washington, D.C., to a member of Congress who has shown leadership and support of library issues. Its awards for Friends groups annually total more than $15,000 and recognize outstanding community and volunteer involvement.

The mission of FOLUSA is to motivate and support state and local Friends groups across the country in their efforts to preserve and strengthen libraries, and to create awareness and appreciation of library services by

- Assisting in developing Friends groups in order to generate local and state support
- Providing guidance, education, and counsel on issues and concerns relevant to Friends and libraries
- Promoting the development of strong and effective library advocacy programs
- Serving as a clearinghouse of information and expertise
- Establishing locations of historical literary significance around the country as Literary Landmarks
- Promoting reading and literacy through a nationwide Books for Babies program

FUND-RAISING

CD Reference: Donations and Membership

This most basic premise of Friends groups, raising money for the library for nonbudgeted items to supplement its funding, can encompass many different forms. Fund-raising can be as elemental as having large jars for change donations placed on store counters. Worms, a variety of other animals, and people have raced to raise money. The idea of what the money is being raised for must be made relevant to the Friends group that is being asked to raise it. If library patrons have to wait too long to check out a best seller, raise money to purchase that book with a jacket cover noting that the book is made possible by a donation from the Friends. If there are not enough computer stations in the library, raise money to purchase extra ones with a plaque on them noting they are a donation from the Friends. Get publicity for what you accomplish. Fund-raising can be expensive, but people who cannot afford to make donations can give their time instead, and can cut expenses by helping with mailings, phone calls, ideas, and other volunteer support. They can speak with their neighbors and local businesses about the need for donations with the help of an **issue statement.** The Friends group cannot always be asking for money, or it will be seen as an elite organization. There must be a balance between fund-raising and programs so that many feel welcome. Special bowling tournaments, Scrabble tournaments, bingo games, all can help the library and be fun. This is one area where thinking outside the box is an asset; you can never tell what will alert a new audience to the potential of the Friends. (See **Capital campaigns; Corporate support; Donations; Grants**)

FUND-RAISING, PROSPECT LIST FOR

For any large fund-raising effort, a list has to be prepared of all people that can be considered prospective donors. This should include all past and present Friends and library trustees, as well as significant figures in the community known to have an interest in improving the community. Bankers, builders, chamber of commerce members, politicians, and educators are all fair game. Then there are the quiet citizens who use the library but are not seen as especially strong prospects. They are just as important as the others; not because they may have hidden resources, but because they represent the community that will provide the largest number of donations. While many companies exist that can help run a capital campaign, they cannot assemble this list, which is the heart of the campaign. It must be done locally. That is why good **record keeping** and software are essential, and efficient ways to access the list are also necessary. Many board members belong to various other service organizations and may have access to their lists, or have other contacts who are helpful in assembling these lists. In some communities, cultural institutions like the museum, orchestra, art museum, ballet, or others share their mailing lists for special purposes. The Friends, not the library, should be a part of that effort, if possible. (See **Capital campaigns**)

GENEALOGY

There is a great deal of support available for Friends groups from people who are interested in genealogy. Their great need is for records of the past which are kept in libraries, many of which are now being made available online. The old directories and records in the library are a valuable resource and need special care as they age. The Friends and the genealogists are part of the team that will help the library to preserve this heritage. In many cases funds are provided by the genealogists for extra equipment to read microfilm or for reference works or software that help trace various genealogies. Sometimes they will help establish a separate room for the public to use for research, occasionally with a part-time volunteer to help newcomers start their search. These rooms can become repositories of local materials that would otherwise be lost. In some areas special collections focusing on Asian or African-American materials are formed. (See **Publications**)

GIFT BASKETS

CD Reference: Programs

An auction or raffle of gift baskets is an undertaking that must be carefully planned, with a realistic appraisal of what your Friends group is capable of doing. These events can be small, pleasant ones or they can involve many people and become a major fund-raising event taking several days. The basic premise is to have baskets (which the Friends can provide) that are distributed to local businesses, individuals in the community, or members of the Friends, and ask them to fill them with some special items. These can be defined ahead of time and be based on book titles or a set theme, like Springtime, Patriotism, Singing in the Rain, or Little Women. There is absolutely no end to what can be devised. You might want to set a dollar limit, or encourage homemade products, or something for children. There is no cost to the Friends, except perhaps for the baskets. Or you can ask other businesses and volunteer organizations to fill a basket that tells about their mission and auction these off, again asking for a literary tie-in. These would likely be more expensive, and you can have the baskets displayed at the library for a day or two, and hold a tickets-only preview party to start silent bidding on them. Public bidding at an event the next day should cap off the bidding, with the proceeds going to the Friends to use for the library. These events should generate a lot of publicity beforehand, showing some of the baskets in progress and during the event as well. Winners and donors should be announced in the Friends newsletter.

GIFT POLICY

CD Reference: Policy Manuals

People can be very generous to the library and to the Friends, sometimes inconveniently so. They may have some treasure that they regard as old and valuable and want to donate it to the Friends to use in an auction or sell in the bookstore. Most libraries have a gift policy, but Friends groups may not. It's prudent to have one, so that your used-book room doesn't become filled with moldy books, old *National Geographics*, and out-of-date textbooks. It's also a way not to become a repository for old paintings by family members and other objects that would only clutter up a space. Have a committee that can be a fallback for making these decisions. By contrast, a cash gift is usually acceptable, unless it comes with a request that is inappropriate.

GIFT SHOPS

Friends groups have moved into the retail area in some libraries, where the traffic is strong enough to support a gift shop. This is not something to undertake without a lot of thought and planning. It is important for the shop to be in a high-traffic area in order to allow for impulse buying. There have to be some fixtures to display the merchandise. There has to be someone to order merchandise with the knowledge of what is appropriate. There has to be staffing during the times the shop is open. Firm accounting systems must be in place, as well as an inventory system. It may take some time before the store is profitable, so there has to be sufficient financial backing. The shop's sales may not be tax-exempt, depending on state law requirements. Some libraries have added a small greeting card area in the space where their used books are sold. This can be a good test to see if an audience exists for novelty items before getting too far into the plan. It's important to consult with other libraries in similar locales to check on their success with this type of venture. Some gift shops go so far as to sell new books. This seems to tread a dangerous line, especially if it ruins the relationship between the Friends and local booksellers. The Museum Store Association publishes *The New Store Workbook,* a handbook that is helpful in setting up a shop; and FOLUSA or ALA offices can refer you to libraries that have successful stores. (See **Appendix A**)

GOALS

The **mission statement** is an outline of your Friends group's general goals to support the library. To attain specific annual goals, decisions have to be made by the board of directors about which elements to emphasize, when to do projects during a particular year, and how much of the organization's **budget** should be directed toward each project. **Strategic planning** is necessary for these decisions, since there are many claims on the time and money of the group. Many times groups have general goals in mind, such as improving the children's room in the library, buying a piano, increasing membership, broadening the board of directors, updating the collection with a best-seller book-rental plan (like a McNaughton plan), or raising money and giving a certain percentage of the profits to the library for special purposes.

GRANTS

It is possible to secure corporate and private grants for particular efforts in a community. Many grants have to do with education, literacy, and children. Most of these grants are not large, but they can make a difference. In most communities where certain large national retail chains prosper, you can get information on their grant-making either from the store itself or from the company's website. Wal-Mart, Target, McDonald's, and other national retailers and restaurant chains are just a few examples. Many regional chains also offer this type of help, as do some large local corporations dealing in nonconsumer items. These grants may only be given at certain times of the year, so research is necessary. Some smaller local area stores may be happy to supply in-kind donations that can be used for prizes, or major items such as office furniture or boxes for packing books. Grants are less likely to be given to a Friends group in a city where the company has no local presence. If your community is lucky enough to have a corporate headquarters or a major plant in the area, be sure to consider them as a resource. Their employees live in the area, and the company will want to be seen as trying to improve it for them. (See **Appendix A**)

GRIEVANCES

CD Reference: Policy Manuals

If an employee has a problem that affects the way their job is performed, there should be a way to resolve the problem if it concerns the Friends or the library. It may be caused by miscommunication about who makes decisions, or by misunderstandings with other people. Whatever the cause, there should be a way to resolve grievances, with a set procedure. A chain of command to resolve grievances and a written set of ways to deal with them are both useful.

HISTORIAN

The historian used to be a common board position but is not always used today. It is useful to have a historian, especially when a Friends organization may have been part of a community for many years. There would normally be a collection of photos of events, copies of articles about the group, lists of board members, and other relevant memorabilia (but not including the minutes, which are kept separately by the secretary). These materials would be kept up-to-date, with the help of the entire board. They would be best housed in the library. The historian is an excellent job for a past president or secretary and could be an ex officio position. A historian is especially useful when a new library director is appointed and needs to be briefed on the role of the Friends group.

HONORARY MEMBERS

The category of "honorary members" should be used with discretion. It is meant to honor someone who has played a unique role in the Friends organization or has done a special service. It might be awarded to an author or speaker who makes an exceptional impact. It could go to the mayor, or someone in the community who has done something special that benefited the library or the Friends. For instance, if someone allows the use of a building to house the books collected for a sale, or provides a car for a raffle, it would be appropriate to make them an honorary member of the Friends, and to do it at a ceremony where others will be made aware of it. You might confer an honorary membership on your group's founder, or on the librarian who helped the group get its start.

HOSPITALITY

The Friends should be the warm hand of welcome at all of their meetings and should work to make people feel comfortable. Name tags, refreshments, informal introductions made around a table at a meeting, calling new members, passing a sign-up sheet at meetings or outside a program, and having the board make a point of circulating and welcoming people they don't know will all help strangers feel part of the group. Asking opinions from the audience lets strangers get to know each other. It also allows the board to get to know new members and note those who would be an asset to the board. If the Friends are sponsoring the meeting, then they should set a friendly tone to the atmosphere. Strangers entering the room should leave with the feeling that they have been welcomed.

INCORPORATION   *CD Reference: Legal Necessities*

Articles of incorporation must be filed at the state level in order for a Friends group to seek **nonprofit status** in its state. With these papers you can then file for a federal tax exemption. It is safer to have the papers use the library's address, since the group's officers change. The state may charge yearly fees for the listing, and the fee reminders should go to an address that remains stable. Once you have state incorporation as a nonprofit organization, you will be tax-exempt according to the laws of your state. Before your group has been so designated, you can say on your membership form that "We are in the process of applying for tax-exempt status," so that people will be able to use you as a tax exemption. Once the papers have arrived, you will be incorporated and able to make tax-exempt purchases according to your state and local laws. After the state designation, you will be able to apply for a federal exemption and an **EIN number** (Employer Identification Number), which is needed for many application forms for grants and donations. (See **Tax exemption**)

INSURANCE POLICIES

Most Friends groups are insured in part by the library's insurance policy. However, if book sales or other Friends events are held some place other than the library, it might be wise to look into a liability policy, and to find out if the directors' and officers' insurance is covered by the state. There are policies available for special events on a one-time basis, and the Friends of Libraries U.S.A. offers a policy for Friends members as well. Our litigious society makes it necessary to protect those who are working on behalf of the library. If the Friends group has employee(s) who handle money in any significant amount they can be bonded, which can be an add-on to the directors and officers insurance. (See **Bonding of employees**)

INTERNET

CD Reference: Publications

The growing use of the Internet has become a major element of some Friends groups' agendas. Many Friends groups have their own website, or have a page on their library's site. This is used to give information about upcoming events (which makes it necessary to update frequently) or at least to give membership and dues information, list board members' names and those of award recipients, volunteer opportunities, and the hours of a bookstore.

Searches are easily made on the Internet to find the best price for equipment the group may want to purchase. The Internet also allows you to communicate with other groups about your problems, contacting them individually or on the FOLUSA-L discussion list. Classes on using the Internet and e-mail are also wonderful programs for the Friends to offer, especially to hesitant senior citizens. The Internet is becoming so important a means of communication that the person in charge of your web connections should be considered for a board position if they are interested. This is also a good way to bring in younger members.

Some dedicated volunteers may take on the assignment of researching certain unusual types of books in the library's possession—unusually old editions, signed copies, first editions, or reader's editions—on the Internet. There are websites dealing in these books, and there's also eBay, the online auction site which has become a fallback resource where you can list a book and sell it to the highest bidder. You can estimate the worth of your unusual books by searching for them on the Web at these sites. (See **Appendix A; Book sales, online auction; Book sales, online fixed-price; Book sales, selling online; Publishers' websites**)

IRS: see **Nonprofit status.**

ISSUE STATEMENT

When the Friends are involved in **lobbying** or advocacy on behalf of a particular project, such as a building expansion or a referendum for a tax increase, the library should produce for them a clear statement of what the purpose of the project is, why it is needed, what the impact will be if passed or not passed, how much the project will cost, how long it will take, what disruption it will cause, and why the Friends are supporting it. This issue statement should be clearly written, with no jargon or acronyms allowed, and should be made available to the Friends for their use when discussing the project in the community or even among themselves. Generalities are not adequate when there is a major proposal on the table, nor should there be any uncertainties about why the project is needed. (See **Capital campaigns**)

JUNIOR FRIENDS

Friends of the Library can be young as well as adult. Groups formed among children encourage reading, familiarity with the library, and teach group behavior. There is decision making, discussions, and lots of fun. Friends can help run these groups, and provide funding for special treats. The parents of the children can become potential members of the Friends and their board. The younger children can also interact with **Teen Friends,** and as they mature will be potential members of that group.

LETTER WRITING   *CD Reference: Donations and Membership*

Friends have a real advantage in their role as private citizens. They can individually write to make their views known to the media and legislators. They can help staff tables in the library to ask other patrons to write a letter to their representative. By letting others know that a segment of the population exists that feels strongly enough about libraries to write about it, the Friends are practicing **advocacy.** Librarians and trustees have a vested interest in funding for libraries, and as a result their voices are less effective.

When writing letters, it's a good idea to have a few general descriptive phrases at hand that can explain any complicated material, as well as a handout of names, e-mail, and addresses to whom the mail will be sent for the various voting districts. This will make the task easier. While form letters don't have the impact of individually written letters, all types of letters have some impact.

LIBRARY DIRECTOR

The director of the library can be the most important person in making a Friends group a success. If support is not forthcoming from the library administration or is not enthusiastic, a Friends group is unlikely to get off the ground. Once formed, however, it can often weather an indifferent administration or two. A supportive director can help position a Friends group to be visible to the community and encourage it in its support of the library. Some directors have heard horror stories of Friends trying to run the library, making trouble and brewing dissent. It is up to the Friends to establish a feeling of cooperation and trust. If the library director does not have time to work directly with the Friends, a staff member should be appointed to act as liaison with them. Care should be taken that the staffer understands the role of the Friends, and the library director is supportive of them. If friction develops between the liaison and the Friends, it must be addressed quickly, as it can poison the atmosphere. The role of the Friends does not involve setting policy for the library, which is the job of the director and the trustees. (See **Codes of conduct; Successful Friends Policy**)

LIBRARY LEGISLATIVE DAY

A Library Legislative Day is held in every state, at a time of year designated by the state library association. Friends can have a great impact by undertaking a yearly visit to the state capitol and to their elected representatives on this day. Because Friends are the voters directly involved in library issues but are not employed by the library, their voices will be regarded as very important. A representative or committee from the Friends group can join with librarians to visit the state capitol together and carry a unified message asking for support and update the legislators on conditions "back home." Transportation costs are usually covered by the state association. There is also a national Library Legislative Day organized by the American Library Association's Washington office. It organizes visits to senators and congressmen and holds briefings for the participants, who travel from their states. It is usually held on the first Tuesday in May. Information is available on the ALA website, www.ala.org.

LITERACY *CD Reference: Programs*

Illiteracy is recognized as a major impediment in our society; however, combating it is not the primary reason for the library's existence, and literacy has its own support groups similar to those for libraries. The Friends may find it easy to ally with these groups in their community as part of their community outreach, though, and if the library director agrees, they may buy special materials or other library tools for adult learners for the library collection as part of their annual donations. However, it is important to remember not to dissipate the Friends' goodwill on behalf of the library on another type of cause.

LITERARY LANDMARKS *CD Reference: Programs*

This program, sponsored by the Friends of Libraries U.S.A., designates sites anywhere in the United States as landmarks dedicated to a particular deceased author or authors. Some examples are a birthplace, residence, school, library, grave, or a site that was an inspiration to the writer. Because of the itinerant nature of many authors during the first half of the twentieth century, many hotels and bars served as authors' second homes. Many people are unaware of the literary heritage that may have incubated in their communities years ago. It may take some sleuthing, asking the newspaper librarian to do some searching, and asking longtime librarians or English teachers to discover authors' forgotten footprints in their community. The literary landmark can become a local point of pride, a tourist destination, or the focal point of a literary festival, awards, or a writer-in-residence program. A handsome bronze plaque designates the site.

LOBBYING

The unfortunate pejorative connotations of the word "lobbying" must be disregarded when describing this main occupation of the Friends, which is usually termed **advocacy**. There are negative associations to the activities of lobbyists because of political history and the misinterpretation of the IRS laws concerning nonprofit institutions. With regard to the latter, Friends are allowed to speak in favor of the library, and are expected to as Friends. What they are not allowed to do is tell others how to vote on a particular issue or candidate. IRS Pub. 1828 states:

An organization will be regarded as attempting to influence legislation if it contacts, or urges the public to contact, members or employees of a legislative body for the purpose of proposing, supporting, or opposing legislation, or if the organization advocates the adoption or rejection of legislation

Friends groups may not spend money for this purpose, and they must keep track of how much money and time their group spends—and their use of space in their newsletters or website—on this purpose to make sure they are not using more than the permitted amount for advocacy. Friends groups are allowed to educate, which means showing both sides of an issue and explaining the benefits of each. According to IRS Pub. 1828:

> Organizations may, however, involve themselves in issues of public policy without the activity being considered as lobbying. For example, organizations may conduct educational meetings, prepare and distribute educational materials, or otherwise consider public policy issues in an educational manner without jeopardizing their tax-exempt status.

If it is necessary to engage in a real campaign, the Friends may want to form a separate committee with a different tax designation. It is often assumed that the chief targets of lobbyists are elected officials of the federal, state, or local governments who have input on budget decisions. However, the reality is that Friends speak more often with their legislative aides or secretaries. These are very important figures in the process; they can give or withhold access, pass on messages in a positive way (or not), and work on the library's behalf in their own way. (See **Letter writing; Library Legislative Day**)

LOGO

CD Reference: Publications

A logo is a distinctive design that should be part of any paper or electronic communication used by the Friends: stationery, newsletter, membership cards, website, posters, signs, and bookmarks. It should be so readily recognized that nonmembers will instantly associate it with the Friends. Designs for logos may have to do with the library, featuring an architectural detail, books, computers, a town symbol incorporated into the Friends name, or just about anything that the board agrees upon. A local public relations group can design one, or a member of the library staff may be able to show some ideas to a talented member. The sooner a Friends group adopts a logo, the better.

MAINTENANCE

A Friends of the Library group must be maintained just like any other community treasure. It is unique in its audience, one that encompasses everyone in that most democratic institution, the library. Once the original group that took part in its early formation has dispersed and others have followed, changes in its structure are bound to have occurred, some for better and some for worse. It is necessary to take a realistic look and make sure the organization continues to grow and maintain itself, not losing its momentum. It must continue to generate excitement and leadership and explore new possibilities. It does this by continuing to make new friends and links in the community, and creating its own role. This is done by finding a niche, whether it be a smashingly successful annual book sale or some other type of community event that brings many people together, perhaps at holiday times where special events are planned. These may be pumpkin contests, scarecrow contests, holiday door wreaths for spring or winter holidays, miniature topiary trees decorated with story themes, mystery nights, dinner in the stacks, after-school programs, sponsorship of summer programs, major yearly raffles (a car, a vacation trip, a special dinner catered in the home), and anything else that works and doesn't step on another group's territory. A mother-daughter reading group can lead to a mother-daughter fashion show or movie night. Volunteers can help orient new citizens and their children to the library. A yearly lecture, perhaps funded by a large local firm or a bequest, with a prestigious speaker on a serious subject can morph from a one-night event to include a daytime symposium, media appearances, and follow-up school visits. The newest trend is selecting a single book to be read by the whole community. The Friends should make sure they are part of this undertaking and should involve themselves in a prominent way, whether in a leadership or support capacity. In any event, members should be easily identifiable as Friends of the Library. (See **Positioning; Programs**)

MARKETING

Every facet of the Friends' public exposure is a marketing opportunity that is either taken advantage of or lost. Encouraging people to join the Friends, patronizing the book sales, taking part in award ceremonies, attending meetings: each is marketing the Friends as a viable community organization that knows how to get things accomplished. The Friends may be a volunteer group, but that doesn't mean that their public face shouldn't be as professional as possible. Don't hesitate to take advantage of the expertise available in the community for nonprofit groups. Make your printed materials look as good as possible, and take advantage of **public service announcements** and local newspapers. (See **Cause-related marketing; Media; Positioning**)

MEDIA

The media need to fill vast amounts of airtime and print space, and they also need to demonstrate their local involvement and public interest. Friends groups and libraries need the publicity. It sounds like a perfect plan for cooperation, except that it doesn't always work. The insatiable appetite of the media focuses on news, which can be in short supply with a moderately active Friends group. There are opportunities, however, and if properly presented the media will cover them. It's helpful to find a reporter who is interested in libraries and books and certainly in information technology. When there is an identified contact it becomes much easier to call about coverage. Don't just say we're having a book sale; it's better to add that the local high school pep band will play at noon, or a choir will perform at three o'clock, or that performers will do skits for children at ten o'clock, which will give parents a chance to shop. Give the titles of some exceptional books for sale, give the media an idea of the teams of people working behind the scene for months to get ready. If the group is having a celebrity speaker for an event, prepare a press kit with all the details and a photo if possible. If you partner with some other business, see if they have media contacts. Don't be shy, but don't cry "wolf" either. No news is no news. Having cute kids helps liven up a scene, and pictures of newborns receiving a library card and a Books for Babies package are always a winner. Always remember to say thank you for the coverage, and if the media do you a real favor, remember them when you're giving out awards. They will give that event publicity too. (See **Book sales, media attention**)

MEETING COSTS

When planning a meeting at the library, you are saving many costs by not having to rent a room or set it up. If your program calls for extended hours, you may have to pay for the custodial help who help put on coffee or clean up after you. Usually the Friends provide refreshments that are appropriate. Even if everyone is on a diet, it's nice to have an opportunity to stand around and visit before or after the program. If a fee must be charged to cover the costs of a gathering, be sure it covers all of the expenses; it's usually more than food that's involved. You may not have to reimburse a member for providing the refreshments. If there is extra expense involved it should be reimbursed. Local businesses may be willing to donate refreshments to bring in new customers; don't be afraid to ask and to give them proper recognition in the program. Paper goods beyond Styrofoam cups may need to be accumulated in stock to save expenses. Some people are willing to use their homes to entertain a group, and that is always appreciated. If your group is holding an event away from the library in a home or public building, check out the insurance liability. You may have to take out a rider. Always check for rules about alcoholic beverages.

MEETINGS

An agenda of some type is necessary for any successful Friends meeting, whether it is a board meeting, a meeting of the membership, or a program meeting. The formality of a call to order is a polite way to get everyone's attention, and reminds the audience that they are participating in an organization. That may be the only "business" there is. You can then go on to the program, and end with thank-you's or a more formal "the meeting is adjourned." Minutes should be read at regular board meetings but can be dispensed with at other types of meetings, as can the treasurer's report. Even Friends groups whose only activity is a book sale need to have at least one formal public meeting for the membership to hold elections. Since this is rarely seen as a fun meeting, there is usually other entertainment planned for the event. Other meetings may be for entertainment, programs with authors or book reviews, award ceremonies, or library or community business. (See **Agenda; Annual meeting; Board meeting; Minutes**)

MEMBERSHIP

The membership of a Friends organization can include many categories and types of people. People should have the opportunity to give their dues at many levels, and should be recognized for their generosity. The whole community should be considered as potential members. For a public library this could include not only those who live in the community, but those who have been involved but have moved away. The **dues** should make it possible for students and teens, families, singles, retirees, summer homeowners, businesses, and other organizations (Women's Clubs, Rotary clubs, chambers of commerce, book clubs) to become members at an appropriate level. Membership dues are what keep the Friends going; the annual dues create the basis for the budget. Because of membership's importance to the health of the organization, it should be considered a permanent item on the agenda.

There should always be an opportunity for the public to join the Friends. If you don't feel your membership brochures are doing their job, redesign them. Be sure your newsletter carries a membership form in it and there are copies available in the library. Have one or two membership drives a year, with Friends staffing tables in the library during busy weeks. A banner hanging outside and some special gesture inside will make a difference, even if it's just a small cup of cider in the fall, or the chance to win a donated prize for people who join within a certain time period. Let them know what their dues money goes toward: have a chart available that lists what your donations have been able to acquire for the library. Hold a special membership drive for parents of young children to help bolster a special children's collection, or perhaps do one for the senior population on behalf of large-print books. In an academic library, the membership dues can enhance certain collections that appeal to students or professors who want special materials available. Software and new items that are too expensive for an individual can also be provided to build interest in the library among different groups on campus. The library is a marvelous resource; it just has to remind people that it is constantly renewing itself. (See **Charter members; Honorary members; Membership renewal form**)

MEMBERSHIP, LAPSED

Lapsed members should be given the benefit of the doubt for several months, since it's likely they will rejoin if possible. They may not have noticed the renewal notice, especially if it was bulk-mailed. They may hold off paying charities and dues until the end of the year. Money may have been tight at the time the notice was originally sent. Maybe they're waiting for a special offer. Maybe they're waiting for a personal call. If the membership renewals are all sent out at one time, it should be fairly easy to keep track of the people who haven't renewed, and they can be sent one or two increasingly noticeable renewals. If that doesn't bring a reaction, follow up with a call from the membership committee or someone on the board who knows the person. Even if they don't rejoin, keep their name in a special list on the computer so they can stay on your mailing list for mailings to large groups, future membership drives, or for advocacy purposes.

MEMBERSHIP RENEWAL FORM

A membership renewal form must include all of the information necessary to make it easy for an existing member to rejoin. If possible, the name and address should be printed with space to make changes as necessary, and a warning about when the expiration takes effect should be included. If you have a membership and renewal drive once a year, it is helpful to have an upcoming book sale as an incentive to rejoin quickly. Let members know how their money was spent in the previous year, and any new plans that they will support in the coming year. Be sure and give an opportunity to rejoin at a higher level of support. A personal letter or call to individual members can help the effort.

MEMORIAL

A memorial is a donation to honor the memory of someone who is no longer living. A gift to the library is a lovely way to remember someone: a family member, friend, or colleague. A request to add a book in a certain subject area is up to the library staff to designate, but Friends can maintain the paperwork, which includes thanking the donor, announcing the gift to the family, and filling out the necessary forms to get the process started within the library. A commemorative bookplate placed in the new book with a place for the name of the designee makes the process special. Sometimes there is a column in the Friends newsletter that lists memorial donations made by members, which serves to remind others of this useful way to remember a friend. (See **Tributes**)

MINUTES   *CD Reference: Running a Board*

Once a **secretary** who has agreed to take the minutes of meetings of the board of directors has been chosen, it is a good idea to identify what amount of detail needs to be included in the minutes. There are certain obvious points to include: a list of attendees; additions and corrections to the previous minutes; and the details (including a copy) of the treasurer's report. If the president gives a report it should have the major points listed in the minutes. The gist of committee reports has to be recorded, including budgets, decisions, and problems. The feeling of a general discussion should be reported, but it is usually not necessary to record everyone's comments. New or old business should be entered, as well as any visitor's comments if germane. Since minutes contain the historical records of the organization, they should contain every motion, who made it and seconded it, and if it passed or failed to pass. The minutes should only record official business, not describe the social activities surrounding the board meeting, like "the board adjourned for a delightful supper served by Amanda Smith in her lovely new home." Minutes should be kept in a separate book, usually by the secretary, and each year's collection filed in a designated area, probably the library.

MISSION STATEMENT *CD Reference: Legal Necessities*

When a Friends group seeks articles of incorporation, the group must give a statement of purpose. These few sentences are the mission statement. They are found in the constitution of the organization. They encapsulate the meaning of what the group aims to accomplish, how the group's efforts will be directed, and how the monies collected will be spent. It is usually best to make this a general statement, not too specific. Phrases like "support the (specific) library," "promote reading," and "enhance the community's appreciation of the library" serve the purpose of the Friends without being too binding. The library has to be specified as your primary purpose. This will protect against the misuse of funds, however well-meaning, by future boards. This is also the reason that all board members should promise to abide by the mission statement when they join the board. When trouble occurs on a board, and a board member has a private agenda that works against the library's best interest (as defined by the library director), they can be removed from the board by the executive committee or the full board for not supporting the group's mission. The mission statement is difficult to change, so it should be carefully considered. It can be rephrased to appear on publicity materials if the meaning is not changed. Broad phrases allow the Friends group flexibility in carrying out its mission, since some years may call for the emphasis of activities on volunteer help rather than fund-raising, or on advocacy rather than programming.

The mission statement protects the group against the possibility of using funds, however inadvertently, in a way that does not benefit the library. There are many allied causes that are also tempting to support, like literacy, English as a second language, and scholarship support, but if there is no direct help to the library the funds are not being spent in support of the mission statement.

MURDER IN THE LIBRARY (LET'S ALL PUT ON A PLAY)

CD Reference: Programs

Mystery plays, hokey melodramas, musicals, and dramatic group readings of famous works are all ways to involve the local population in having fun in the library. There's a whole range of materials available, and the Friends group that puts on a "whodunit" may not necessarily be anxious to celebrate Bloomsday and James Joyce, but that's the point. Mothers may decide to put on a musical for small children, and teens may have a talent show or a battle of the bands. There will always be an audience, and the library should profit. Some Friends groups plan these events yearly, so that the whole community comes to expect them.

NATIONAL PROMOTIONS

There are many weeks designated throughout the year that are natural promotions for the library, and also for the Friends, whose programs may support those promotions. A Readathon during Banned Books Week is always a good way to get publicity, depending on the local politics. Children's Book Week is a good time to bring in a children's author or to have a children's book fair. Advocacy is something needed all year round, but is especially expected during National Library Week. There are also literacy-based events, National Volunteer Week, and state and local events. There is the library's birthday, and anniversaries for the Friends group. There are also the One Book One City events, in which the library and the Friends participate.

NEWSLETTER

CD Reference: Publications

Communication with members is the primary factor that keeps Friends groups alive. It lets the membership know that they belong to a group that is active and working for their library. The newsletter has long been that primary link, especially for those who do not visit the library as often as they once may have. The newsletter makes up for not seeing the Friends in action at the library, because it tells about what has been and will be taking place. Some who read about it will want to participate, while some will just think "how great they're doing" and go on with their lives. Some will look for their names to be mentioned for work done, donations made, or a special gift or milestone. The form of the newsletter should show that some care has been taken on it, but it should be in an easy-to-read format with large enough print to be easily legible. At the very least it should be published quarterly. It can be mailed or sent by e-mail, with the choice made available on the membership or renewal form. Extra copies should be made available in the library to draw interest in the Friends group.

Board nominations should be announced in the newsletter, upcoming programs publicized, opportunities for volunteers listed, book sale information given, and book donations solicited. Lists of the people who have contributed money or time or have done a special service should be mentioned.

There doesn't have to be a large staff working on the newsletter if the board and the library staff learn to contribute their material on a regular basis. E-mail will make it easier, since the editor would be able to paste the material sent to her into the document. It is possible the library will help with the printing, or an outside service can easily do it. With computer technology photos are much easier to use, although not necessary. The Friends' contact information should be on the newsletter, as well as the Friends' logo to make it easily recognizable from other pieces of mail. (See **Bulk mail; Publications**)

NOMINATING COMMITTEE   *CD Reference: Nomination Process*

The nominating committee is an extremely important committee, and the members of it should be carefully chosen. Its purpose is to nominate new members to the board of directors who will help the Friends organization grow stronger and enhance its position in the community. The people that join the board should have skills that will be helpful in the future activities of the board, which may be somewhat different each year, within the context of support for the library. The committee should analyze several determinants before beginning the nominating process. They must first see whose terms are due to expire, whether any have the option of remaining on the board if asked, and if that would be a good move or not. They have to determine if the vice president is willing to succeed the president if the president will not remain in office. Will the secretary and treasurer stay in office? How many of the board members have terms expiring or have reasons to leave the board?

Once you know the vacancies that have to be filled, you are in a position to begin the nomination process. First make a grid, if you have not done so already, that shows you the characteristics of those remaining on the board. These might include any special talents, contacts, skills that have proven useful, and the community the members represent, whether cultural, age, gender, or ethnic. Which region of the city are they from? Once you have these questions answered, it will show you what areas need some help. Do you have contacts to business on the board, links to various other helpful groups, to the media, and a lawyer or an accountant? Someone with public relations experience or fund-raising skills, or links to the city government? This exercise will help you narrow down your search. It is hoped that the committee collected possible nominations to the board during the year, and that other board members have offered names as well. To fill a leadership position, it is best to look at the existing board if the vice president is not able to move up to president. Someone with board experience and an organizational background is helpful. Whether a dynamic personality is required or not is also important to decide. (See **Board members, recruiting; Elections**)

NONPROFIT STATUS

If your Friends group becomes a nonprofit organization, it does not have to pay federal or state corporate taxes or state sales taxes. Corporations and individuals that make donations to these organizations can deduct their contributions from their income tax. To be so designated, an organization must first be incorporated at the state level as a nonprofit, and will be exempt from state taxes, and depending on local laws, from local taxes. Donations to it will also be exempt from state tax. Its constitution must limit the organization's purposes to an exempt purpose, including education and supporting the library. It may not be political (see **Lobbying**).

To become a nonprofit organization, your Friends group must have a ruling from the IRS, which you must apply for by filling out the form(s) discussed below, copied from the IRS website (www.irs.gov). When successfully applied for, the organization receives an **EIN number** which signifies its status as nonprofit and is used as its identification number, and which donors use to claim tax deductions. All IRS documents are available online, and there is explicit plain language to guide you through the process. The key documents are IRS Pub. 557, "Application for Recognition of Exemption"; IRS Form SS4, "Application for EIN" (Employer Identification Number); and IRS Form 1023, "Application for Recognition of Exemption and Instructions Form 872C." (This last document provides an advance ruling contingency so that taxes will not have to be paid prior to the ruling.) You will need a conformed copy of your group's constitution (or "articles of organization") to apply. You can apply by telephone for an EIN number, but must have a filled-out form available to you when you call.

Don't be afraid of the IRS website. It has clear instructions, written in clear language. It is a vast improvement over the former incomprehensible maze it once was. Go to www.irs.gov; in the far left column click on "Information-Charities and Non-profits"; in the far left column click on "Information-Charitable orgs." You can also do a search for the numbers of the publications and forms given above.

Applying for nonprofit status is not too onerous a job if you have all of the necessary documents available. There are items in these documents that will help you include the correct information in your Friends group's constitution, which you must include with your application as well. It might prove helpful to divide the sections of these documents among several members to begin with and go over them together at the final stage. (See **Incorporation; Tax exemption**)

Charities and Nonprofits Exemption Requirements

The organizations described in IRC Section 501(c)(3) are commonly referred to under the general heading of "charitable organizations." Organizations described in IRC Section 501(c)(3), other than testing for public safety organizations, are eligible to receive tax-deductible contributions in accordance with IRC Section 170.

The exempt purposes set forth in IRC Section 501(c)(3) are charitable, religious, educational, scientific, literary, testing for public safety, fostering national or international amateur sports competition, and the prevention of cruelty to children or animals. The term charitable is used in its generally accepted legal sense and includes relief of the poor, the distressed, or the underprivileged; advancement of religion; advancement of education or science; erection or maintenance of public buildings, monuments, or works; lessening the burdens of government; lessening of neighborhood tensions; elimination of prejudice and discrimination; defense of human and civil rights secured by law; and combating community deterioration and juvenile delinquency.

To be organized exclusively for a charitable purpose, the organization must be a corporation, community chest, fund, or foundation. A charitable trust is a fund or foundation and will qualify. However, an individual or a partnership will not qualify. The articles of organization must limit the organization's purposes to one or more of the exempt purposes set forth in IRC Section 501(c)(3) and must not expressly empower it to engage, other than as an insubstantial part of its activities, in activities that are not in furtherance of one or more of those purposes. This requirement may be met if the purposes stated in the articles of organization are limited in some way by reference to IRC Section 501(c)(3). In addition, assets of an organization must be permanently dedicated to an exempt purpose. This means that should an organization dissolve, its assets must be distributed for an exempt purpose described in this chapter, or to the federal government or to a state or local government for a public purpose. To establish that an organization's assets will be permanently dedicated to an exempt purpose, the articles of organization should contain a provision ensuring their distribution for an exempt purpose in the event of dissolution. Although reliance may be placed upon state law to establish permanent dedication of assets for exempt purposes, an organization's application can be processed by the IRS more rapidly if its articles of organization include a provision ensuring permanent dedication of assets for exempt purposes. For examples of provisions that meet these requirements, download Publication 557, Tax-Exempt Status for Your Organization.

An organization will be regarded as "operated exclusively" for one or more exempt purposes only if it engages primarily in activities which accomplish one or more of the exempt purposes specified in IRC Section 501(c)(3). An organization will not be so regarded if more than an insubstantial part of its activities is not in furtherance of an exempt purpose. For more information concerning types of charitable organizations and their activities, download Publication 557.

OFFICE SUPPORT

As a Friends group grows and prospers, the work involved in keeping up the mailings, the membership list, and the financial records also grows. Usually, the first staff that's hired by a group is a part-time administrative assistant who helps with these tasks. Sometimes the Friends can pay part of the wages of a library employee for a few extra hours of work each week. It is likely that eventually the administrative job will become a full-time position. This person should not be a member of the board of directors. (There should be a provision in the bylaws that no member of the board can benefit financially from the Friends group, since this would be seen as a conflict of interest.)

Once the Friends office is staffed (see **Executive director**), there may be other areas that suggest the need for paid employees. These might be a used-book store or gift shop that has grown large enough that volunteers are no longer adequate to keep it running efficiently; or a book fair and author event that has expanded from an hour-long visit and chat with a small audience to become a major community event. Someone with experience can make these programs more efficient and should be able to make enough money to pay for their salary and still make a profit. A volunteer coordinator is another position that may be shared with the library in some cases; this person helps fill many of the slots available for volunteers.

PARADES

CD Reference: Programs

Civic parades with marching bands and floats are good opportunities to increase the visibility of both the Friends and the library. Often the summer reading program will have a float in the Fourth of July parade, with a reading theme and the children participating, sometimes by handing out bookmarks or library pins and other promotional materials. There are similar promotions for local or state fairs: places where the Friends can staff a booth for the library and give out reading lists for different needs. Libraries in towns with large summer vacation populations that swell the local crowds can take advantage of this by selling items on their lawn if they're well situated, or by staffing a lemonade or special refreshment stand. In some communities, library drill teams have shown great unexpected skill. Armed with nothing more than matching outfits and book carts, they often make the evening news broadcasts.

PARTNERS, BUSINESS

Businesses like to be associated with good causes; it is up to the Friends to give them the opportunity to do so. There should be categories for businesses on your membership brochure, or perhaps on a special brochure for businesses listing the sponsorship perks that might be available for them. Keeping in mind that there are mom and pop businesses as well as large corporations that could help the library, it might be helpful to consider the value of gifts in-kind and make small businesses that donate goods and services members or honorary members of the Friends, so they get the benefit of being listed in your materials. Minimum values should be set for this recognition, depending on the size of the businesses. (See **Cause-related marketing; Corporate support; Donations**)

PAYPAL

PayPal is an especially useful way to collect money for dues and tickets and make other financial collections from your members and donors. It enables any individual or business with an e-mail address to securely, easily, and quickly send and receive payments online. (See **Appendix A**)

PERKS

Giving a premium, such as a coffee mug or bookbag, for a membership donation is not necessary, but allowing members to come to a book sale preview is always a positive perk, as is an invitation to view some special exhibit with an expert, or to visit with a speaker before or after a program. Many bookstores have made arrangements to give members of the Friends a discount, which is also a membership perk. This type of perk must be negotiated.

PLANNING

Planning is intrinsic to the success of any Friends organization. There must be **strategic planning** (long-term planning), program planning, and budget planning. From these plans all else flows: budgets, committees, events, programs, awards. Once something is planned, it can always be revised as reality intrudes. (See **Budgets; Programs**)

POSITIONING

"Positioning" is a marketing term. When you position a product (or an organization) you are staking a claim in the mind of your audience. (For example, McDonald's occupies an emotional territory that evokes food, fun, and family.) If the position your Friends group has chosen turns out to be ineffective, you need to reassess the needs of your audience and find a position that will be more relevant to them. You might take a written survey of your members in your newsletter, and ask their favorite activities from your group's past year; be sure to list them. If you don't get an adequate response, try a phone survey of a random sample group. If most of your members are just paying dues and not attending events, try and find out what they would like. Your members may prefer daytime programs if they're seniors, or more child-centered events if they're young families. Nostalgia movie nights might be fun for some families. For an adult audience there might not be time for much except an occasional author event or just book sales. You must determine how important programs are in gaining members; the ones you have may not be relevant. If you are providing volunteer opportunities, advocacy information, and have fundraising opportunities in place that are effective, your Friends group is healthy. The book sale and its preview are incentive enough for most members. (See **Evaluation of programs; Maintenance; Programs**)

PRESIDENT

The president of a Friends group, besides presiding over the board of directors meetings, typically represents the group at other public functions both at the library and in the community, attends official library meetings, and attends local community budget deliberations on behalf of the Friends to speak on behalf of the library. It is helpful if the person chosen for this position is comfortable being in the public eye, and does not have too many personal commitments that preclude these obligations. It is sometimes hard to get someone to assume this role, so some groups have established copresidents, or split the role between two people for half a year each. Members of local corporations will often take on the role, since it is a service to the community and a way to show involvement, as well as good public relations for their company and a good entry on resumes and press releases. Sometimes the vice president is able to help out with some of the president's duties, and certainly other members of the board can step in to help when needed. The ideal term of office for a president is difficult to assess. Within a group that has a minimal number of activities, it will be fairly easy for a person with previous organizational experience to catch on quickly, so a one-year term may be adequate. In a more complex situation, a person may find themselves just hitting their stride at the end of the year, and may wish to serve more than a year's term. Assuming that the board and membership are pleased with the choice, your bylaws should be able to accommodate these possibilities. One way would be to have one-year terms that can be renewed for two or three years. There should be adequate turnover in this position, as in any other.

PROGRAMS

CD Reference: Programs

Programs are of major importance to any Friends group. The program chair is usually in charge, with a committee, of one-time programs during the year. Year-round activities like the bookstore, gift shop, or volunteers usually have individual chairs. Annual events like tree decorating or pumpkin-carving contests can be handled as a program or special event. The board of directors is usually very free with ideas for programs, but the hard part is deciding if they will work in your community or if they are practical. The question should always be, what will the Friends and the library gain from the effort required?

Excellent records must be kept of the programs you've held, both those that were successful and those that were not. It's important to know what worked and what didn't, how much it cost, where it was held, and whose services were required. The IRS and other groups whose forms you fill out like to know what programs were held by your group. Did they relate to your mission statement? Members of your board should attend programs as often as possible. Be sure to invite library trustees and local politicians to attend; if they do, introduce them to the Friends group. Invite the library director to say a few words at a program if possible.

Something very simple might become a popular annual or regular program. A librarian discussing new books added to the collection on a quarterly basis, or a column in the newsletter listing new books that have arrived, make the point that the library is not a static institution. A monthly program given by members who describe their travels to interesting places has proven popular. Mother-daughter programs, while the girls are still young enough to enjoy it, have led to interesting book discussions. A year-long effort by Friends to encourage parents to read to children is a program that brings credibility to the group. Funding a storyteller who appears on a regular basis is another program that can touch many young lives and be worthwhile. A used-book store, ongoing volunteers for library projects, after-school homework helpers, visiting authors, book groups, lunchtime travel programs, breakfasts for business people, award events, and contests are just some of the programs that are undertaken by Friends groups. (See **Evaluation of programs; Maintenance; Positioning**)

PROGRAMS, BOOK-RELATED

CD Reference: Programs

Small communities may not be able to hold many author programs, but the demand continues to grow for book-related programs. Most Friends groups plan programs for their members where they can socialize and share common interests. Programming is becoming more difficult because of so many working families with little discretionary time, except in places with a strong retiree population. However, working with a local bookstore to promote an author appearance or a discussion of current best sellers helps expand the audience, is an opportunity to recruit more members, and relieves the Friends of some of the work involved in these programs. Most important are the opportunities to showcase new literary talent and to provide information to those who are interested in becoming writers and learning about the mechanics of publishing. Workshops can be held with the help of local faculty, people in the community who have published, and arrangements with publishers who have authors in the area. Given the popularity of **book clubs,** a number of authors have begun to communicate with their fans by e-mail, chat rooms, or long-distance group calls. Friends groups can hold a program with a live author via the Internet or e-mail. Much of this sort of information can be found on **publishers' websites.**

PUBLIC RELATIONS: see **Marketing.**

PUBLIC SERVICE ANNOUNCEMENTS

Public service announcements, or PSAs, are brief announcements that are made available by your local broadcasters. These announcements are not something to overuse; save them for special events, such as a large book sale or some other large public event. If you're lucky there will be some slow news days when your PSA will air in a good time period. Otherwise, your spot may be relegated to late night or early morning. The National Association of Broadcasters makes available a pamphlet, *Getting Your Message on the Air,* which includes tips and ideas on how to approach your local broadcasters to get your message on the air. You can access their site at www.nab.org/publicservice.

The Federal Communications Commission (FCC) offers the following information about PSAs, which is in its Code 73.1800 but is no longer accessible on its website:

> The FCC does not have a radio or television public service announcement guide. There is no specific requirement as to the amount of time a broadcast licensee should devote to public service programming.

The licensee is expected to serve the needs and interest of his/her service area and to provide programming which in fact constitutes a diligent effort, in good faith, to provide for these needs and interests.

However, within this broad framework the licensee has the obligation to decide which type of programs, including announcements, are presented.

Individual radio and television station licensees are responsible for selecting all broadcast matter and for determining how their stations can best serve their communities. Licensees are responsible for choosing the entertainment programming and the programs concerning local issues, news, public affairs, religion, sports events, and other subjects to be aired by the station. They also decide how their programs, including call-in shows, will be conducted and whether or not to edit or reschedule material for broadcasting.

The FCC does not substitute its judgment for that of the broadcaster in this process, and it does not act as an advisor to stations on artistic standards, grammar or quality of content.

Every broadcasting facility has to have its FCC license renewed on a timely basis. At that time they ask for letters from their listeners to document their community involvement, or ways they can improve. On its site on "The Public and Broadcasting" the FCC writes: "We license radio and TV stations for a period of up to eight years. Before we can renew a station's license, we must first determine whether it has served the public interest."

PUBLICATIONS   *CD Reference: Publications*

There are many opportunities for publications beyond the ubiquitous **newsletter,** which is almost obligatory for a Friends group. (Some groups now offer a choice of sending their newsletter by either snail mail or e-mail.) Some groups produce an annual report describing their past year and including names and photos. This can be part of the Friends newsletter, or part of the library's newsletter, or it can be a separate publication. Some of these become very elaborate, and some very amusing; they do take time, thought, and financing.

Friends members have a wide range of interests, and there may be some not on the board who would like to work on a project that could end up as a publication. These publications could include histories of a period in the town's past; chronologies of the history of the library; memorable past events such as a natural disaster or a war; comparisons of ethnic migrations to the town, or of census statistics; famous people that came through the town, including authors; and photos from the library's collection. Some of these materials can form the basis of pamphlets, stationery, or calendars. Publication projects can be especially meaningful when a centennial or other anniversary is about to be celebrated. At times they prove so popular they become annual publications. In a town that has a large tourist population they can become keepsakes of a vacation, such as a yearly calendar. Then there are always the widely popular cookbooks that reflect a regional bias, featuring the best local home cooking and some well-known local restaurant treats. (Just be sure to have a committee that checks each recipe.) Other types of publications can include children's stories and drawings based on their library story hours and made available to their parents with the Friends help.

Still other types of publications can be more high tech. A collection of screen savers for computers, available on a CD of current and historical photos of the community, is especially nice as a graduation gift or a gift for tourists and former residents. Other ideas include putting historical documents or former city directories that would be useful for genealogists on a CD that could be purchased on the Friends' website. This may sound difficult but is not, using present-day technology. It's also a good way to bring in younger people who are so familiar with this technology. There could also be a publication that the whole town can work on, but that does not get published. Instead it is started in the library with a few sentences that sound like something out of a romance novel, but set in the local community. It should be publicized so as many people as possible add to it, and publicly read after it is finished, and perhaps kept on display for a while. Often this is done at Valentine's Day. Some Friends groups sponsor publications of poetry or short stories for their community on a yearly basis, using local people to judge which entries to include. Other publications include **brochures** containing information about the Friends, and **bookmarks,** which can hold original haiku verse composed by members, as well as information.

PUBLISHERS' WEBSITES

Publishers' websites can give you information about reader's guides, author visits, and news about favorite authors. They are constantly updated. They will also alert you to special promotions and the online availability of their writers. Some publishers' sites are listed below. If you don't find the name of one you're particularly interested in, enter the publisher's name listed on the book on http://www.google.com/ and go to the site listed.

Random House, Inc., http://www.randomhouse.com/—Click on "Trade Services," then "Libraries," and you will find many options.

HarperCollins Publishers, http://www.harpercollins.com/—Click on "Reading Groups" and you'll find many services and programs your Friends group can use.

Penguin Group (USA) Inc., http://penguinputnam.com/—Click on "Browse," "Reading Guides," "Newsletters."

W.W. Norton & Company, http://www.wwnorton.com/—Click on "General Interest Books," then choose from the list.

Algonquin Books, www.algonquin.com/—Click on "Library Resources" for information on reading guides, authors, and books.

Workman, http://workman.com/—This site provides information on the popular Book Lover's Calendar.

QUORUM

A quorum is the minimum number of members necessary to hold a meeting or cast a binding vote. There must be a quorum present to elect officers and board members and to change bylaws at the annual meeting. A percentage of the total membership is a good way to express this number, rather than giving a number which may prove impossible to fulfill.

RAFFLES

CD Reference: Legal Necessities

The term "raffle" as used in this entry can also be expanded to include silent auctions and auctions. A raffle is a wonderful way to raise money for the Friends if it is not overdone in your community and, of course, if it is allowed in your state (to check, look up the name of your state and "raffles" online). It seems that every state has different regulations covering raffles and auctions, but permits are usually necessary, and there are probably some limitations on how many can be held in one year. Once the legal considerations are addressed, the rules governing the event must be determined, dates picked, and good prizes decided upon. Tickets for raffles are available from party stores that sell decorations and supplies. They are also available online. Gift baskets are a popular raffle item, as are other assortments of items donated by local stores. Goods and services from members, time in vacation cottages, donated travel packages, clothing, jewelry, tickets to special events, and autographed books have all been successful prize items. If you have a popular author or filmmaker in your area, they may be willing to add a gift of using the name of the raffle winner as the name of a character in their next book or movie.

RECOGNITION   *CD Reference: Donations and Membership*

One of the most important elements of working with an organization of **volunteers** like the Friends is recognition of those who donate their time, money, resources, talent, and enthusiasm. This can be done in a number of ways, but it must be done. It can be as simple as saying thank you publicly at a meeting. It can be a list of names posted at the library or book-sorting room. It can be a box in your group's newsletter with a special mention in it, or an article describing the efforts made. If it might help for others to know, as in the case of a student helper, a letter for their file sent to the school would be appropriate. In the case of city workers, letters to their department head are important. In the case of young business people, it is important for their business to be identified, so that their name is associated with the name of their employer in any publicity. Their firm should also be thanked. A state Friends of the Library group should give appropriate thanks to those who help make state policy for libraries (if appropriate) as well as to the various local groups that help them in their activities. At the end of a term of office, there should be a significant thank-you said to the outgoing Friends president and other officers. An additional group that is exceedingly important consists of the library and legislative staff people who don't ordinarily get recognition but do much of the work, taking messages, making appointments, answering phones, setting up chairs and tables, etc. (See **Awards**)

RECORD KEEPING

Any organization accumulates records. What they are and how they are used is important for the health of a Friends group. Financial records are kept in a secure place and are accessible only to the treasurer and accountant. Just like personal tax receipts, they are the proof of expenditures for the organization and should be kept as long as recommended by the accountant. It is good to let your members know every five years or so how much has been donated to the group, and toward what projects. A list of donors should be kept forever. Even if a donor stops giving, they might resume giving later if approached, or be called on for special projects, or honored for past generosity. Membership lists are also useful, even if some are lapsed. When advocacy issues arise, these known library supporters should be informed. Awards should also be tracked to be sure there is equity in the way they are given in the community over the years. A record of the people who served on the board of directors over the years is also helpful, particularly when questions arise about the way something was done.

If these materials do exist in print, the library is the best place for them to be housed. For the short term, personal computers are fine, but eventually old records should not be kept privately. The longer a group is in existence, the more meaningful its past becomes. When it comes time to write a history of the group, there should be multiple sources to draw upon, including a collection of all old newsletters and annual reports. (See **Document storage**)

RESOURCES

There are many resources not immediately visible that can help a Friends group. First and foremost of them is the library director, who may not wish to intrude on the group but may also have some very good ideas. The second is Friends of Libraries U.S.A. (FOLUSA), a national association of local Friends of the Library groups, and the publisher of a newsletter and a discussion list that are fantastic opportunities to share ideas and questions with peers. There are the local chamber of commerce, various groups in the art or cultural nonprofit area, and citywide networks of various kinds that provide opportunities for learning about organizations, leadership, programs, funding, and other core interests. Since you belong to a library group, you might consider asking the reference librarian to help you find groups that might be kindred spirits. Or ask personal contacts if they are familiar with such groups, or the city hall, which may have a list of these groups. There is a wonderful opportunity twice a year to meet Friends from all over the country at the **American Library Association** conferences. They are held in different regions of the country in major cities, and FOLUSA holds its own mini-conference within them. This allows for one-to-one conversations, panel discussions, and workshops, all aimed at the Friends. These contacts increase morale levels geometrically. **State libraries** and **Center for the Book** groups are other resources to consider. The *Friends of Libraries Sourcebook* is also a good resource and is available at your local library. See **appendix A** for a list of resources available on various websites.

RESUMES

CD Reference: Nomination Process

Your Friends group should keep a file of applications for positions on the board of directors and for prospective employees. Life changes can decimate a board suddenly, and it is always good to have replacements in mind. When filling a paid position for help, select a committee with experience in hiring to handle this task. It is important to check resume references, and to understand that the answers given by former employers may hold hidden meanings about the job applicant.

REWARDS

There are many organizations, private and public, that recognize outstanding work by an individual or an organization. Very often, Friends of the Library fall in a gray area because they are not regarded as specifically helping literacy, children, or education, some of the current hot topics. That is only because the general public is not aware of how Friends and libraries benefit everyone, no matter by what definition. If a program has been a success for several years and fills one of the criteria of an award, nominate your Friends group for it. Even if you don't win, you will make others aware of the good your group has done and will raise the group's profile. Not only programs but leaders are also recognized by various groups. If your Friends group has an outstanding president, program chair, or committee chair, try and enter their name for an opportunity to be recognized. Each community has both civic and private organizations that present community awards, as well as corporate groups that recognize community movers and shakers. Consider the outstanding volunteer awards, business awards, chamber of commerce awards, Rotary awards, Point of Light awards, mayoral awards, Kiwanis, etc. If someone in your group is nominated for an award, be sure they are interviewed. Radio, television, and local cable stations, as well as the press, often interview local people as part of their community outreach. Keep them informed about potential speakers in the group. (See **Awards; Recognition**)

SCHOLARSHIPS

The money raised by the Friends is for the betterment of the library. Often the Friends will give a scholarship to a library worker who wants to advance his or her education in the library field. It is usual to have a contract or promise that once their education is finished they will return to the library, but that may be difficult to enforce. It is easier to give grants to them to attend workshops, classes, conferences (state or national), or seminars if there is some benefit to the library.

Friends can also give an allowance to their own board members to help them attend a state or national (FOLUSA) conference to learn about the programs of other Friends groups. Sometimes Friends want to thank high school volunteers, and give money toward their college education. This seems a deviation from the mission of the Friends, since it is not strengthening the library in any way, except for the goodwill from the recipient's family.

SECRETARY

CD Reference: Policy Manuals

The position of secretary in a Friends group entails much more than writing down what was discussed at the board of directors meeting. In effect, the secretary keeps the history of the organization by means of the record established through the **minutes.** Every motion made by the board is recorded, every report by the treasurer is kept, and a record of whether motions were passed or defeated is maintained. Who made the motion is noted, and who seconded it. The secretary's signature is recorded on the copy of the minutes that are submitted. Minutes are distributed to the board, and each year's minutes should be gathered to be kept at the library. The minutes also note who was in attendance at the board meeting, and who was absent. The secretary is also part of the **executive committee** and takes minutes at those meetings as well. If the secretary is not able to attend a meeting, an acting secretary is appointed. At some meetings, a tape recording is made to help the secretary compile accurate minutes. They are transcribed later.

SOFTWARE

Some Friends groups are able to use the regular software that comes bundled in their computer for their record keeping and publications. Some need more advanced software to track a large membership and donor base. These decisions have to be made on a case-by-case basis. It is helpful to get on the Web or phone and find out what Friends groups in similar situations use, or what those that are larger need. If older software is still being used, it would be wise to upgrade. There have been major improvements that will relieve a lot of drudgery from the chore of keeping membership lists up-to-date.

SPEAKERS, FEES FOR

The many types of speakers that may participate in Friends-sponsored programs and events will all have different ways of determining if or how much they will charge for their time. This must be clarified before they step through the door. Make clear if you have no funds, or can only afford a token honorarium. Offer hospitality, a dinner out with a few people, or drinks or dessert afterwards. Find out if they expect you to cover the cost of lodgings or meals. See if there is another group that would like to cosponsor the program and share the costs. It is often possible to have a donor underwrite the program, in honor of something, or just for the business publicity. If the speaker is an author selling books, their publisher will often cover the costs, while expecting the Friends to make every effort to sell lots of books. If the speaker is a civic figure or a local expert, a membership in the Friends or a donation to the library in their name is thoughtful. Placing a book in the library in their name is always an appropriate gesture; it should be in a field related to the speaker's area of expertise.

STATE AND LOCAL REQUIREMENTS

Don't automatically take anyone's opinion about what has to be done to fulfill your Friends group's legal requirements for anything unless they practice law: incorporation, raffles, bingo, auctions, fund-raising, dues, ticket sales, bus trips, driving others in cars, holding events off-site, changing bylaws, anything that might include a regulation. It is difficult to know what each local government requires; they are all different, and each state may have a different department in charge of the function. Luckily, it is easy to check for yourself. Once you get on the state website, you will find many options and, luckily, phone numbers. Usually you can just enter a keyword and the information is provided, but you may have to call and ask for help in finding the information. The phone numbers are usually toll-free. Researching the requirements is a task easily divided among your group's officers or a committee. Local and state representatives also maintain offices that provide information and support.

STATE FRIENDS OF LIBRARIES

Most states have a network of Friends groups within them, usually made up of public library groups, but occasionally with academic Friends groups as well. They are helped to communicate with other groups by the state library or the state library association. State library association conferences also provide an opportunity for Friends to meet, but it may be expensive for individuals to afford to attend and pay for registration and housing. They often meet at a local library instead of renting a room. It is difficult to keep statewide Friends groups active because of the expense and travel needed to attend meetings. It is typical to move around the state to include all regions. Those who do attend find it very gratifying to share their ideas, and to help other areas find ways to involve themselves in the state group. Statewide groups usually give awards made to different-sized chapters, with the awards sometimes underwritten by statewide businesses. Awards are also given to legislators and for media coverage, and outstanding Friends are recognized as well. Programs such as **Literary Landmarks** are often used to bring attention to the group's annual meetings. A Friends statewide newspaper allows groups to share in the information without attending the meetings, while e-mail, videoconferencing, and conference calls allow some useful interaction. A list of active statewide Friends groups is provided in **appendix B** of this book and in the attached CD, and another such list is available from the Friends of Libraries U.S.A.

STATE LIBRARIES

Most state libraries have a consultant within their structure whose job includes working with Friends of the Library groups. Because these consultants must know the libraries in their state, they also know if they have Friends of the Library groups and have been important in bringing them together, giving workshops for them or helping them form state Friends of Libraries. The consultants are a wonderful, if overworked, resource, and getting to know them will be very useful. They can be especially helpful when it comes to advocacy issues, lists of libraries that have Friends groups, and other information that is collected statewide. The state librarian can also be a great resource, once made aware of the needs of groups. The state library will most likely be able to set up long-distance conferencing workshops for Friends groups in large states that have far-flung populations.

STEERING COMMITTEE

A steering committee is assembled by citizens who are interested in forming a Friends of the Library group. New groups are often formed with the support of the library director, who can help identify those who could be helpful to the group. Some on the steering committee are not always interested in serving on the board, but may have contacts in business or politics that are useful. The steering committee helps formulate a preliminary mission statement, constitution, and bylaws that lead to the election of the first formal board of directors. In some cases seed money is needed, if the library is unable to absorb the initial expense of starting the group. These funds can be provided by an "angel," a larger, more established Friends group in the community, or another organization like the PTA, Rotary club, or Women's Club. (See **Committees**)

STRATEGIC PLANNING *CD Reference: Running a Board*

Strategic planning is long-range planning undertaken by the board to position the Friends organization and rededicate it to its mission. The planning takes into consideration outside factors that may influence these decisions (such as changes in the community), looks at the board's makeup, and examines how current programs fit into the organization's goals. It may find that things taken for granted for years no longer apply. It may find new opportunities that exist. Strategic planning can be an exhaustive process stretching over a long time period, or it can be the subject of a daylong board retreat. A planning retreat should be conducted by someone outside of the board with experience in the process. (There may be a service in the community that provides help of this nature to nonprofit groups.) Work is usually done ahead of time to bring together the information needed to have an informed discussion. The planning retreat can be viewed as a once-a-year doctor's checkup, or as a refresher for the group, or as a way to decide if a new project should be undertaken and how it should be done.

SUCCESSFUL FRIENDS POLICY *CD Reference: Policy Manuals*

Every Friends group has moments when its members wonder why they are working so hard if no one appreciates what they are doing. There are always points of friction because of the close relationships between the groups that work on behalf of the library. Working to avoid these tensions is part of being a successful Friends group, and the Successful Friends Policy below will help mitigate the hard times.

- The library director must approve the concept of a Friends group. It is counterproductive to continue the effort if approval is not forthcoming.
- The library staff that is assigned the job of working with the Friends must be willing to do so.
- Those involved must understand the commitment of time and energy involved.
- The library and the Friends should have an agreement about which library resources will be available for use: space, staff time, paper, phone.
- A core group of citizens who are interested in the Friends should be involved. In some instances a core group may be only two or three people.
- The authority to which the library director reports should be aware of the Friends.
- The full library community should be made aware of the Friends; there should be no hint that all are not welcome.
- All those involved in the Friends must realize that the Friends group does not make library policy, but supports it. The trustees decide the library policy, along with the library director. This does not include the Friends.
- The library director works with the Friends to have their activities emphasize the changing needs of the library each year: advocacy, social, fund-raising, volunteers, morale, etc.
- If the Friends have their own 501(c)(3) nonprofit status, they may decide on how the funds they raise should be disbursed, according to information provided by the library director. If they do not have their own EIN number, the funds may be used by the library or the local government.

SUNSHINE LAWS

CD Reference: Legal Necessities

All states, the District of Columbia, and the federal government have open meeting laws, requiring agency officials to hold certain meetings in public.

These laws do not necessarily ensure that members of the public will be allowed to address the group, but they do guarantee that the public and the media can attend the meetings. Check your state's law to be sure of the requirements.

TALENT SHOW

There is a type of talent show where everyone is a winner, and there is always an audience. Children under six or seven years are adorable no matter what they do, or what they think their talent is. They have relatives that think so too. Charge a nominal admission, have a program with the participants' names in it, someone who can play the piano, and some emergency supplies in case mothers forget them. (See *Murder in the Library*)

TAX EXEMPTION

It is very desirable for a Friends organization to be a nonprofit, and thus be tax-exempt. It can then go ahead and file for an **EIN number** for federal tax exemption, so that its donors will be able to make federal tax-free donations of money or supplies to the Friends group. If the gross annual receipts of the organization are less than $25,000, it does not have to file an IRS Form 990. However, to encourage the community to make donations, being tax-exempt is necessary. While there is an expense to filing for **nonprofit status,** this can be a significant aid to bring in donations and memberships. A Friends group can raise money before being granted nonprofit status if they note—on their membership forms, for example—that their application for it is in process. If the group does not have its own EIN number and is raising money using the library's number, the money raised can become a contentious issue; it has been known to be claimed by the local government for its own use, or by the library trustees for capital funds, and the Friends are left with their projects unfunded. (See **Incorporation**)

TECHNOLOGY

Friends groups are often asked to underwrite the purchase of new items of technology for the library that can't be accommodated by the library's capital budget. Especially at times when budgets are being cut, technology is seen as a frill. Unfortunately, the public doesn't always understand this, and feel it is their right to have technology available in the library. This can be a plus for the Friends, since they are seen in the role that best fits them, as providing and helping the library. It also provides an excellent reason to raise money for an easily perceived need. This can also set off a discussion among the Friends about what technology is really needed, and what types and brands are best to buy. While it is likely that someone will know a way to get "a better price" than another, and someone else will have an opinion about whether the library should have DVDs or videotapes added to the collection, and someone else will say it's silly to spend money on a technology that may soon be obsolete, these decisions are best made by the library director, who may ask for ideas, but will know what is actually needed in terms of the collection.

TEEN FRIENDS

High schoolers need to show community involvement on their school records, employment applications, and on their college applications. Their organization into Teen Friends of the Library can be of great help to the library as well. They can form reading advisory groups, help shelve books, work with younger patrons doing homework help, help with Junior Friends, and help adults learn how to use the library's computers. It is also useful to have a high school representative on the adult Friends group's board of directors. (See **Board members, recruiting**)

TERM OF OFFICE

The length of a term of office on the board of directors or as president should be carefully considered. If it is not stated, and there is no way to rotate the people serving on the board, the Friends group will stagnate, and keep others from becoming active. Rest assured that good people who love the library will continue to work for it once they are off the board. Bringing in new people to join those already working on behalf of the library should be a continuing goal of the group. Sometimes a faction will "take over" a Friends organization and eliminate its competition from the board. In these cases having the term of office in writing becomes more valuable. A copy of the constitution and bylaws should be on file in the library at all times and the library director should have a file copy. As years go by, new staff and new members of the community come in who are unfamiliar with the

Friends, and they should be able to acquaint themselves with the organization by reading old newsletters and the documents of organization. It is also vital that the library director be aware of the bylaws in case the Friends board veers away from the mission statement of the organization. The Friends group is a public institution, and these documents are legally available to the public. (See **President**)

TREASURER

CD Reference: Policy Manuals

The treasurer is an elected officer of the board of directors. The treasurer's term of office may be longer than that of other officers in a Friends group, for the sake of continuity. The treasurer's **record keeping** duties may include paying bills; maintaining accurate records of financial transactions; and depositing dues and other funds and negotiable instruments in the name, and to the credit, of the organization in such depositories as the board may designate from time to time. The treasurer pays all bills through checks drawn on the account of the organization and signed by designated officers. No money beyond that which is formally budgeted may be spent in the name of the organization without prior approval of the board. The treasurer is a member of both the executive committee and the finance committee. The treasurer prepares financial reports of income and expenditures for all meetings of the board and quarterly reports for the finance committee chair, president, and the executive director. The treasurer also presents an annual financial report to the membership at the annual business meeting. The treasurer assists the accountant or personally makes timely financial reports to the Internal Revenue Service and other agencies as required by law. Investments are made in consultation with the finance committee and financial professionals.

A Friends group's **finances** may be fairly simple early in the life of a group, but as activities increase, and as laws change and impinge on the actions of the group, the treasurer's responsibilities increase accordingly. A lay person can handle this post if there is a certified public accountant overseeing the process. A **budget** for a small Friends group can easily be handled with a simple computer program like Quicken or Money. Once there are employees, QuickBooks is very helpful for keeping track of taxes and deductions. The larger the Friends group becomes, the more complex the record keeping becomes; donations have to be tracked from year to year, mailings done on a regular basis, and the membership records kept current. (See **Document storage**) While these are not the job of the treasurer, the records themselves are important as backup to keeping the group's financial accounts accurately.

The treasurer's report is one of the first items on the agenda of a board meeting, because it is like a thermometer for measuring the health of the group. After the money situation is clear, plans for activities can be made in keeping with the bank account. The treasurer gives a report at every board meeting, or sends one if unable to attend, and gives a yearly report at the annual meeting. The reports given are part of the permanent minutes of these meetings. The treasurer helps inform the **fiscal policy** decisions of the board.

When picking a candidate for treasurer, the nominating committee might try to enlist the help of one of the major accounting businesses in town, or one of the major banks (where your group might deposit its funds). It is likely that a young officer or an interested Friend employed there will take on the job of treasurer as a community service. Care should be taken to write letters of appreciation on their behalf to the employers. The commitment needed to fulfill this job properly is a great gift to the Friends group.

TRIBUTES

A Friends group can raise money for the library and raise public awareness of the library's supporters by instituting a program that allows patrons to make donations to honor or memorialize individuals. Those honored should be notified that a donation has been made in their name, or that their name will go on bookplates placed in appropriate books. This process works well for birthdays, graduations, good report cards, special accomplishments, new babies, etc. An appropriate book is chosen that is to be part of the library collection, and a bookplate is placed in it with the appropriate name. The process has to be worked out with the library staff. The Friends should handle the correspondence that informs the giver and recipient of the choices made. Sometimes there is a column in the newsletter that lists donations made by members in this way, which serves to remind others of this useful way to honor a friend. (See **Memorial**)

TRUSTEES

CD Reference: Running a Board

The trustees are the policy-making or advisory arm of the library, and work with the library director. Library trustees may be elected or appointed, paid or unpaid. Their work is different than that of the Friends, and should be kept separate. The boards of the two groups should not overlap, although a representative of each board may be liaison at the other's board meetings. Communications between the two boards should be friendly and supportive. Most trustees belong to the Friends anyway. Very often, Friends become trustees, or trustees become Friends when their terms expire. (See **Codes of conduct; Control**)

VICE PRESIDENT *CD Reference: Policy Manuals*

The post of vice president can be thought of in several ways. It can be a way to keep someone valuable to the group involved, or it can be recognition of the high regard they're held in. It can also be regarded as a training ground for the role of president, and is often thought of as the president-elect. The vice president steps in to assist the president, such as attending meetings to represent the organization and presiding over the board if the president is away.

VOLUNTEERS *CD Reference: Volunteer Management*

Volunteers are a precious resource for any Friends group. Ranging from members of the board to a children's story hour helper, they may devote hours every day or only a few hours each year, but together they can produce tremendous accomplishments for their chosen organization. Friends volunteer activities have introduced many people to each other, and to the wonderful feeling of working on behalf of a worthy cause. Volunteers should be treasured, thanked, and nurtured. Younger people should be made partners in the Friends enterprise; students and children of members should be recruited as volunteers whenever possible. Some volunteers prefer not to attend Friends meetings, or to be actual members; this is the way they feel independent, but are nonetheless to be considered part of the mix and included in thank-you events. It is not possible to have the predictability of an employee with a volunteer, but there are ways to try and regulate their efforts. Book sales may draw a loyal group that works together and becomes a family, having lunch together, working especially hard prior to a sale, and coming together for years in this way. This is a wonderful testament to the benefits of a collaborative working environment. However, these groups can become too close-knit, and must be made aware of the necessity of staying available to newcomers of different ages and backgrounds. Members should be made aware of the volunteer opportunities available to them, through the newsletter and membership form. The worst way to handle this is to offer an opportunity for volunteer work and then not call on the people who sign up. The best way is to contact them and tell them how the volunteer process works, and give them choices depending on their situation. Many hidden talents will be uncovered and new avenues of opportunity opened if the Friends group is responsive to volunteers. (See **Recognition**)

WEBSITE: see **Internet.**

Appendix A
RESOURCE WEBSITES FOR FRIENDS

Abebooks.com, www.abebooks.com—On this site you can buy and sell new, used, rare, and out-of-print books.

Amazon.com, www.amazon.com—Online bookstore.

American Booksellers Association, www.bookweb.org—The site with the freshest news about bookstores and national and regional meetings of the ABA.

American Library Association, www.ala.org—For promotional products, go to the "ALA Online Store"; check for dates of national promotional events, such as National Library Week, and check to see if there is an ALA conference being held near you. By clicking on "*American Libraries,*" the monthly magazine published by the ALA for members is available through this site. The magazine's January and September issues carry information about housing and transportation to ALA conferences.

Antiquarian Booksellers of America, www.abaa.org.

Barnes & Noble, www.barnesandnoble.com.

BookExpo America, www.bookexpoamerica.com—This site will guide you through the vast convention that showcases the books that will be published in the coming year. It is the best place to find out what authors will be available to tour to promote their new books, and to get the contact names necessary to make the arrangements. Many librarians attend this event.

ChooseBooks.com, www.choosebooks.com—You can ask your members to buy new and used books through this site, including international, independent, new, and used bookstores and library stores. Your group earns 4 percent of any sales credited to your group.

eBay, www.ebay.com.

Friends of Libraries U.S.A., www.folusa.org—The first place to check for information on Friends of the Library groups.

Half.com, www.half.com—EBay books, textbooks, and audio books.

Home Depot, www.homedepot.com—Gives volunteer help, most likely in building projects. Look under "Corporate Responsibility," "Social Responsibility." The best bet might be in renovating a bookstore or a small building project for the children's room.

In My Book, www.inmybook.com—Stylish greeting cards that turn into a bookmark, all with sly book-related puns; these are perfect to sell in bookstores, at book sales, or to use as thank-you notes for your volunteers and donors.

Independent Sector, www.independentsector.org—This site provides information on factors that encourage people to donate and volunteer.

Institute of Museum and Library Services, http://www.imls.gov—An independent federal grant-making agency dedicated to creating and sustaining a nation of learners.

Library BookSales, www.librarybooksales.org—This site lets Friends and libraries list books for sale individually, and allows buyers to contact them; it includes tips on how to evaluate, price, and sell out-of-print and rare books. There is a chat room, an events calendar, newsletter, etc. The cost is a 10 percent commission based on the sale price of the book.

Library Journal, www.libraryjournal.com—This site is a resource not only for librarians but also for those interested in new library technologies and publishing trends. It can also guide you to regional conferences where you can plan to meet other Friends.

Library Media and PR, www.ssdesign.com—This site contains helpful public relations tips and material for libraries, and links with the ALA.

Library of Congress, State Libraries, http://lcweb.loc.gov/global/library/statelib.html—This site has links to all fifty state libraries.

Lions Clubs International, www.lionsclubs.org—Standard grant brochures and applications are available here. The support of your local Lions chapter is crucial to the success of an application. These grants are available to expand services for disabled and visually impaired persons using assistive devices.

Museum Store Association, www.museumdistrict.com—Resources for museum stores, and a conference for members with vendors that can have some materials relevant to library stores.

National Association of Broadcasters, www.nab.org.

Oriental Trading Company, Inc., www.orientaltrading.com—"Stuff" for any occasion and any age: crafts, activity materials, costumes, accessories, novelty jewelry, party supplies, small toys and games.

PayPal, www.paypal.com—This eBay company enables any individual or business with an e-mail address to securely, easily, and quickly send and receive payments online.

Points of Light Foundation & Volunteer Center National Network, www.pointsoflight.org—This site includes lists of volunteer centers. The page www.pointsoflight.org/nvw/ gives specific information about National Volunteer Week, which is a good time to recognize those that help your organization.

Stumps, www.stumpsparty.com—Parade and float information and novelty items.

Target, www.target.com—At the bottom of the home page, click on "Community Giving" listed under "Company," which lists their interests, including childhood reading.

TechSoup.org, www.techsoup.com—A national tech resource guide for nonprofit groups. Includes many helpful discussion areas and sources.

Tutor.com, www.tutor.com—One of many services that provides tutoring help online in libraries.

U.S. Toy, www.ustoy.com—Novelties for every holiday or event.

Wal-Mart, www.walmart.com—The best bet is its Community Matching Grants program, especially if you have a Wal-Mart employee involved.

Appendix B

STATE FRIENDS OF LIBRARIES ORGANIZATIONS

The following list provides contact information for statewide Friends of Libraries organizations. For more information about state Friends groups, send an e-mail to janerutledge@earthlink.net.

Alabama
Friends of Alabama Libraries
No current information

Alaska
No information

Arizona
Arizona Library Friends
1333 East Ellis Drive
Tucson, AZ 85719-1939

Arkansas
Friends of Libraries Arkansas
5000 Cliff Drive
Fort Smith, AR 72903

California
Friends & Foundations of California Libraries
11045 Wrightwood Place
Studio City, CA 91604
http://www.friendcalib.org

Colorado
Colorado Library Association Trustees and Friends Division
No current information

Connecticut
Friends of Connecticut Libraries
786 S. Main Street
Middletown, CT 06457
http://www.cslib.org/focl

Delaware
Friends of Delaware Libraries
P.O. Box 1319
Bethany Beach, DE 19930-1319

District of Columbia
Federation of Friends of DCPL
1423 Iris Street NW
Washington, DC 20012

Florida
Friends & Trustees Interest Group
c/o Florida Library Association
1133 West Morse Boulevard, Suite 201
Winter Park, FL 32789

Georgia
No information

Hawaii
Friends of the Library of Hawaii
690 Pohukaina Street
Honolulu, HI 96813-3185

Idaho
No information

Illinois
Friends of Illinois Libraries
200 West Dundee Road
Wheeling, IL 60096-2799

Indiana
Friends of Indiana Libraries
c/o Library Development Office
140 N. Senate
Indianapolis, IN 46204
http://www.incolsa.net/~foil/

Iowa
Iowa Library Friends
No current information

Kansas
Friends of Kansas Libraries
901 N. Main Street
Hutchinson, KS 67501
http://www.skyways.org/KSL/fokl/

Kentucky
Friends of Kentucky Libraries
No current information

Louisiana
Friends of Libraries of Louisiana
No current information

Maine
Friends of Maine Libraries
64 State House Station
Augusta, ME 04333-0064
http://www.friendsofmainelibraries.org/organizations/foml

Maryland
Citizens for Maryland Libraries
P.O. Box 267
Funkstown, MD 21734-0267
http://www.citizensformarylandlibraries.org

Massachusetts
Massachusetts Friends of Libraries
29 Fairchild Drive
Holden, MA 01602
http://www.masslib.org/mfol/

Michigan
Friends of Michigan Libraries
1200 S. Canton Center Road
Canton, MI 48188
http://www.foml.org

Minnesota
Minnesota Association of Library Friends
1619 Dayton Avenue, Suite 314
St. Paul, MN 55104-6206

Mississippi
Friends of Mississippi Libraries
1221 Ellis Avenue
Jackson, MS 39209
http://www.mlc.lib.ms.us/advocacy/friends/index.htm

Missouri
Missouri Trustees and Friends Council
c/o Missouri Library Association
1306 Business 63 South, Suite B
Columbia, MO 65201

Montana
No information

Nebraska
No information

Nevada
No information

New Hampshire
Association of New Hampshire Library Friends
No current information

New Jersey
New Jersey Friends of Libraries
This organization has disbanded

New Mexico
No information

New York
Empire Friends
c/o New York Library Association
252 Hudson Avenue
Albany, NY 12210-1802

North Carolina
Friends of North Carolina Public Libraries
4640 Mail Service Center
Raleigh, NC 27699-4640

North Dakota
No information

Ohio
Ohio Friends of the Library
c/o Ohio Library Council
35 E. Gay Street, Suite 305
Columbus, OH 43215
http://www.olc.org

Oklahoma
Friends of Libraries in Oklahoma
c/o Tulsa City-County Library
400 Civic Center Tulsa
Tulsa, OK 74103
http://www.okfriends.net

Oregon
No information

Pennsylvania
Pennsylvania Citizens for Better Libraries
604 Hunt Club Drive
Greensburg, PA 15601
http://www.pcblpa.org

Rhode Island
Rhode Island Coalition of Library Advocates
No current information

South Carolina
Friends of South Carolina Libraries
P.O. Box 11121
Columbia, SC 29211

South Dakota
No information

Tennessee
Friends of Tennessee Libraries
P.O. Box 158623
Nashville, TN 37215-8623
http://www.friendstnlib.org/

Texas
Friends of Libraries and Archives of Texas
P.O. Box 12927
1201 Brazos
Austin, TX 78711

Utah
No information

Vermont
No information

Virginia
Friends of Virginia Libraries
c/o LVA
800 East Broad Street
Richmond, VA 23219-1905

Washington
Washington Library Friends, Foundations, and Trustees Association
4016 1st Avenue NE
Seattle, WA 98105-6502
http://www.wla.org/wlffta

West Virginia
West Virginia Friends of the Library
No current information

Wisconsin
Friends of Wisconsin Libraries
2367 S. 84th Street
West Allis, WI 53227-2501
http://www.cheesestate.com/friends

Wyoming
No information

Bibliography

Dolnick, Sandy, ed. *Friends of Libraries Sourcebook.* 3rd ed. Chicago: American Library Association, 1996.

Levin, Lillian, and Friends of the Welles Turner Library. *Planning Library Friends' Book Sales.* 2nd ed., updated and expanded. Order from the Friends of Connecticut Libraries, 786 S. Main St., Middletown, CT 06457.

McCracken, Linda D., and Lynne Zeiher. *The Library Book Cart Precision Drill Team Manual.* North Carolina: McFarland, 2002.

Reed, Sally Gardner, and Beth Nawalinski. *Making Our Voices Heard: Citizens Speak Out for Libraries.* Three-part Powerpoint CD-ROM and workbook in English and Spanish. Philadelphia: Friends of Libraries U.S.A., 2004.

Reed, Sally Gardner, Beth Nawalinski, and Alexander Patterson of Friends of Libraries U.S.A. *101+ Great Ideas for Libraries and Friends.* New York: Neal-Schuman, 2004. (Call FOLUSA directly for special Friends pricing.)

Robert's Rules of Order. 10th ed., newly revised. Reading, MA: Perseus, 2000.

Sturgis, Alice. *The Standard Code of Parliamentary Procedure.* 4th ed. New York: McGraw-Hill, 2000.

Windwalker, Stephen. *Selling Used Books Online: The Complete Guide to Bookselling at Amazon's Marketplace and Other Online Sites.* Belmont, MA: Harvard Perspectives Press, 2002.

Sandy Dolnick is the nation's leading expert on volunteer support for libraries. As the founder and newly retired executive director of Friends of Libraries U.S.A. (FOLUSA), she has spent her career advocating and aiding the efforts of community volunteer supporters of libraries. Upon becoming its executive director in 1985, Dolnick built FOLUSA into a comprehensive program of education, information, and advocacy on behalf of libraries. FOLUSA has grown twentyfold over the last 15 years to encompass more than 2,000 Friends groups and one million members in all 50 states. Dolnick is the editor of a number of publications about libraries, including the popular *Friends of Libraries Sourcebook*.